Papa Joe's Letters

A Collection of Musings, Words of Wisdom and Thoughts on Life

PAPA JOE LUBBEHUSEN

ISBN:1484978390
ISBN-13:9781484978399

DEDICATION

This book is dedicated in loving memory to my departed dear sweet wife Marjorie Rose.
She was the love of my life for 57 years and will always be in my thoughts and prayers.

It is also dedicated to my three wonderful children, John, Sally, and Sara who have always been by my side, day by day, in times of need and to my departed daughter, Susan, who will always be remembered with love.

ACKNOWLEDGMENTS

I would like to thank Jack Telfer who always gave me a venue to voice my thoughts, who encouraged me to write and then printed my letters in the Midland Daily News. I consider Jack to not only be a great editor and a wonderful man, but a true friend. Thank you Jack.

FORWARD

Over years past, as I aged into my golden years, I found myself writing. It began on the beach in Naples, Florida and grew from there. I started out by writing stories of my life growing up. These I would give to my grandchildren, I thought, and I did produce three binders for each of them. But then it progressed to letters to the editor with my words of wisdom, thought, and musings on life and all that I had learned.

I hope you enjoy reading my letters as much as I enjoyed writing them, imparting my words of wisdom on the world, the only way I knew how, through letters to the editor.

So remember folks, "Don't sweat the little stuff, and everything is little."

Love from Papa Joe

Letters from Papa Joe

Smell the Roses – September 7, 2000

To the editor:

Being retired, my wife and I have an opportunity to regularly walk, shop and drive around our town. During these outings we have an opportunity to observe many things.

We truly enjoy the nice things we encounter, but there are also things that can be somewhat distressing at times. So, this morning after one of our walks, instead of getting uptight about the unpleasant things we encountered, I decided to compile a list of "I believe life would be less stressful":

- If people would park between the lines designated in parking spaces.
- If motorists would refrain from using cell phones while driving.
- If young motorists who can hardly see over the steering wheel wouldn't drive so fast.
- If motorists would refrain from driving with a cigarette in one hand and a soft drink in the other one.
- If people would trim the trees that hang over the sidewalks.
- If people would remove dead tree branches and other debris from the walkways.
- If people who walk their pets would clean up their doo-doo, especially on the sidewalks and in my yard.
- If supermarkets would have a lane for cash payments only.
- If supermarkets would have a lane for credit card and check payments only.
- If supermarket clerks would refuse a cart full of groceries in a lane for 10 items or less.
- If, when totaling my golf score, the results wouldn't be so astronomical.
- If all of the above wouldn't be so frustrating to me!

They say that as people get older, they get grouchier. That is not true! We are all born that way, but when we get older, we don't give a darn and say what we want to!!

Have a great day and don't swear the little things!!

Lighten Up, Enjoy Life and Watch Out for Those Polka Dots – October 31, 2000

To the editor:

Recently I wrote a letter to the editor sharing some opinions on "I believe life would be less stressful if …" and proceeded to list a number of those situations. Since then many friends have told me how much they enjoyed reading those adult truths of life.

Well, guess what, I recently ran across an article (author unknown) that gives a child's perspective on the truths of life. This amusing and informative little tidbit is titled "Great Truths About Life That Little Children Have Learned":

1. No matter how hard you try, you can't baptize cats.
2. When your mom is mad at your dad, don't let her brush your hair.
3. If your sister hits you, don't hit her back; they always catch the second person.
4. Never ask your 3-year-old brother to hold a ripe tomato.
5. You can't trust a dog to watch your food.
6. Don't sneeze when someone is cutting your hair.
7. Reading what people write on desks can teach you a lot.
8. Puppies still have bad breath, even after eating a breath mint.
9. Never hold a vacuum and a cat at the same time.
10. School lunches stick to the wall.
11. Don't wear polka-dot underwear with white shorts – no matter how cute the underwear is.
12. You cannot hide a piece of broccoli in a glass of milk.

One final comment. "I believe life would be less stressful if more people would lighten up, smile, be happy, enjoy life and don't sweat the little things."

Truth About "Real Moms" – May 11, 2001

To the editor:

During the past year I have submitted some "time honored truths of life" of little kids, adults and most recently senior citizens. Now that Mother's Day will be here soon, I would like to submit for your edification, some time honored truths of life about "real moms." I hope you enjoy them.

- Real mothers don't eat quiche, they don't have time to make it.
- Real mothers know that their kitchen utensils are probably in the sand box.
- Real mothers have sticky floors, filthy ovens and happy kids.
- Real mothers know that Play Dough doesn't come out of shag carpets.
- Real mothers don't want to know what the vacuum just sucked up.
- Real mothers sometimes ask "why me?" and get their answer when a little voice says, "because I love you best."
- Real mothers know that a child's growth is not measured by height or years or grade – it is marked by the progression from mama, to mommy, to mom.

Happy Mother's Day to all of you wonderful moms.

Just a reminder to all of you out there who might have forgotten, Mother's Day is Sunday. Give yours a big hug and a kiss and tell her how much you love her. She'll really like that!

Tips for the 2001 Graduates – June 6, 2001

To the editor:

Since this is graduation season, I would like to extend my congratulations to all of you graduates. I would, if I may, also like to offer you some words of wisdom that I read some time ago. The gentleman who wrote them pointed out that there are two types of education – the one you receive in school and the one you get in life. Put them together and you have a lot of wisdom.

The trouble is, some people don't figure out what's going on until after half their life is over. So to help educate graduates without them having to go through all the trials and tribulations and hard knocks of life, I would like to pass on some of these pearls of wisdom. Pay attention, this is the last final exam.

- Don't sweat the small stuff, and remember most stuff is small.
- Nobody is indispensable, especially you.
- People are more important than things.
- If you wait to have kids until you can afford them, you probably never will.
- People who do the world's real work don't usually wear neckties.
- A good joke and laugh beats a pill for a lot of ailments.
- There are no substitutes for fresh air, sunshine and exercise.
- A smile is the cheapest way to improve your looks, even if your teeth are crooked.
- May you live your life so there is standing room only at your funeral.

Dads Deserve Some Time Too – June 12, 2001

To the editor:

Last month for Mother's Day I submitted a letter highlighting some time-honored truths of real moms and tried to answer the question, when is a mother a "mom."

Well, Father's Day will soon be here and I think I would be remiss if I didn't give him equal time. So our question today is: When is a father just "Dad?" I have heard this question answered something like this:

- If he's wealthy and prominent and you stand in awe of him, call him "Father."
- If he sits in his shirtsleeves and suspenders at ball games and picnics, call him "Pop."
- If he tills the land or labors in overalls, call him "Pa."
- If he wheels the baby carriage and carries bundles meekly, call him "Papa" with the accent on the first syllable.
- If he belongs to a literary circle and writes cultured papers, call him "Papa" with the accent on the last syllable.
- If, however, he makes a pal of you when you're good and is too wise to let you pull the wool over his loving eyes, when you're not, and you're sure no one else you know has quite so fine a father, you may call him "Dad."

I once read a little ditty by B.C. who explained what a father was in a little different way. It went something like this:

Some people call their daddies "Dad" and some just call them "Him," others call him by his name, just like he's one of them. Some call him "Pop" or "my old man" and some just call him "Pa," but one thing one should never do, is call him late for dinner. Ha!!

Finally, in my ode to mothers I suggested you give her a big hug, kiss and tell her you love her. I don't know about the kiss part, but I still suggest you give your father a big hug and tell him you love him. Go ahead, I'm sure you will both feel good about each other – and yourself!

There are Lessons to be Learned in School – September 11, 2001

To the editor:

School days! School days! Gold ole Golden Rule Days! Yep, school has started again and so has the advice from the younger generation.

Last year, I submitted a letter to the editor giving a child's perspective on the truths of life. One of those truths was "Don't wear polka-dot underwear with white shorts – no matter how cute the underwear!"

Guess what? My school teacher daughter has just passed on to me some more of those "pearls of wisdom," which I would like to pass on to your readers. I hope they enjoy them.

- When you get a bad grade in school, don't show it to your mom when she's on the phone.
- Felt markers are not good to use as lipstick.
- Don't pick on your sister when she's holding a baseball bat.
- Never tell your mom her diet's not working.
- Never allow your 3-year-old brother in the same room as your school assignment.
- Stay away from prunes.
- Never squat with your spurs on.
- When your dad is mad and asks you, "Do I look stupid?" Don't answer him.

And finally, some good advice from a gray haired mature citizen. "Be really nice to your friends, because you never know when you are going to need them to empty your bed pan and hold your hand."

In the meantime, keep a smile on your face, be happy, enjoy life, and please, don't sweat the little things!

Pray One for Joe – September 22, 2001

To the editor:

Yesterday, after church services, I was on my way to my favorite restaurant for my usual Sunday brunch. On the way, I passed one of the local golf courses and noticed quite a few golfers – both men and women.

My first thought was "look at all those poor souls playing golf on Sunday instead of being in church." But, being the compassionate and understanding Christian that I am, I decided to give them the benefit of the doubt. I told myself, "They probably went to a Saturday church service, or they were going later today after their golf game, or maybe they went to church this morning before their golf game." (Quite a dreamer aren't I?)

I know it is none of my business if people go to church or not, but I would like to offer a suggestion – just in case! How about when you golfers come off the 18th green, instead of and before going into the 19th hole for a refreshment, why don't you take a few minutes for a quick impromptu prayer – spikes and all!

If you had a good day golfing, you can bow your head and thank the good Lord for hitting all those long and straight drives, accurate chips and sinking all those long putts.

If, on the other hand, you had a rotten day, you can look up to heaven and ask the good Lord to forgive you for all those nasty things you uttered after hitting all those poor shots. You might also ask him for better guidance on your next golf outing.

Soon, it will be too cold, (for many people!) to play golf, and then you can turn your attention to getting dressed up and going to church on Sundays.

Contrary to a recent article in the MDN regarding "Fewer people getting dressed up for worship service," I adamantly believe that people should get dressed up for worship services! You don't have to get dressed to the max or get consumed with physical appearance, but going to church in those ill-fitting shirts, shorts, jeans, sandals and all that other casual clothing is inappropriate and an erosion of values.

You would not wear those clothes to your boss's house, would you? Well, when you go to church, you're going to visit God in His house and He definitely is a lot more important than your boss!

So whatcha say? The next time you go to church, how about putting on some nice, decent looking clothing? I'm sure you'll feel a whole lot better about yourself and how you look. (Your fellow parishioners might also like the way you look!)

More than anything else, just remember to go to church and when you go, please say a prayer for old Papa Joe – I can use all the help I can get.

More Great Truths – December 6, 2000

To the editor:

Recently I wrote a letter to the editor submitting some comments on "Great Truths About Life That Little Children Have Learned." Evidently a lot of people enjoyed it as I have received many favorable comments.

I concluded my letter with an editorial comment for people to "lighten up, be less stressful and don't sweat the little things." In other words don't worry!

Well, guess what? I just found another informative little tidbit that illustrates or summarizes my comments. I hope you enjoy it. It's entitled: Why Worry?

There are only two things to worry about – either you are well, or you are sick. If you are well, then there is nothing to worry about – but if you are sick, there are two things to worry about – either you get well, or you will die. But if you die, there are only two things to worry about. Either you go to heaven or to hell. If you go to heaven, there is nothing to worry about. If you go to hell, you'll be so darn busy shaking hands with old friends, you won't have time to worry.

So, whatcha worrying for? Like I keep saying, "Smile – lighten up, enjoy life and don't sweat the little things."

Stupid is Not a Politically Correct Word – July 1, 2001

To the editor:

Recently, I got somewhat of a lesson on social etiquette while visiting my 6-year-old and 8-year-old grandchildren. (They prefer "going on 7-years-old and 9-years-old, Papa Joe!") If they only knew what was ahead, they wouldn't hurry to get so old so quick!

Anyway, evidently in one of my highly intellectual dissertations on some earthshaking matter, I somehow or other used the word "stupid." I quickly learned that I should not use that word in front of my grandchildren. They quickly informed me that, "Papa Joe, that is not a very nice word and you should not use it!" Out of the mouths of babes!

So, what do we call someone, who in our estimation does not meet our intellectual standards? If we shouldn't refer to them as stupid, maybe we can circumvent it by using a supposedly more politically correct name. I have come up with a few examples for your edification that should not offend anyone – especially my grandchildren. The person:

- Is a few clowns short of a circus.
- A few beers short of a six pack.
- Doesn't have all his cornflakes in one box.
- Is a Fruit Loop shy of a full bowl.
- The cheese slid off his cracker.
- The wheel's spinning but the hamster's dead.
- Doesn't have all his dogs on one leash.
- Elevator doesn't go all the way to the top floor.
- His antenna doesn't pick up all the channels.
- Missing a few buttons on his remote control.
- Receiver is off the hook.
- In the pinball game of life, his flippers are too far apart.

I would like to make one final comment regarding "stupid" and it concerns the upcoming July Fourth holidays. Many people will be traveling to and fro visiting family and friends, and unfortunately, sometimes some people have a tendency to drink and drive.

I would like to pass on this piece of wisdom to those of you who will be on the highways during the holidays: "He who comes forth with a fifth on the Fourth – may not come forth on the fifth."

So, I say unto you – if you drink and drive, you are stupid! And that's the truth!

Lighten Up – August 14, 2001

To the editor:

Many years ago before retiring, I used to write a monthly business report and to spice it up, or try to take the boredom out of reading it, I used to incorporate a bit of humor.

Recently, while going through some of my old files, (yes, I'm a pack rat!) I found some of those old inspirational proverbs I used to put in my reports. Here's a few for your perusal – I hope your readers enjoy them.

Doing a job right the first time gets the job done. Doing the job wrong 14 times gives you job security.

We put the "k" in "Kwality."

Rome did not create a great empire by having meetings – they did it by killing all those who opposed them.

If something doesn't feel right, you're not feeling the right thing.

Teamwork means never having to take all the blame yourself.

Never underestimate the power of very stupid people in large groups.

Hang in there, retirement is only 30 years away.

Go the extra mile – it makes your boss look like an incompetent slacker.

When the going gets tough, take a coffee break.

Succeed in spite of management.

We waste more time by 8 a.m. in the morning than other companies do all day.

Eagles may soar, but weasels don't get sucked into jet engines.

I'm sure most of these proverbs are still applicable today in the modern business world, the same as my philosophy of life is: "All of our lives would be a lot less stressful, if we would lighten up, smile, be happy and don't sweat the little things."

Be Happy and Don't Sweat the Small Stuff – April 5, 2001

To the editor:

Before I headed south to "warm up" I submitted a couple of letters to the MDN editor highlighting some "truths of life" both from an adult and child's point of view.

While down here doing my beach duty (making sure no Russian submarines attack our beach!) some of my fellow snowbirds and I did a lot of philosophizing, and we came up with some senior "time honored truths of life."

I am sure my friends back home will be happy to know that I have been exercising my mental capabilities and not just basking in the sun. As such, I have decided to share with everyone some of those time honored truths of life.

- The older you get, the better you realize you were.
- Age is a high price to pay for maturity.
- Women like silent men – they think they're listening!
- Do pediatricians play miniature golf on Wednesday?
- If you ate pasta and antipasta would you still be hungry?
- Before they invented drawing boards, what did they go back to?
- Do infants enjoy infancy as much as adults enjoy adultery?
- If the No. 2 pencil is the most popular, why is it still No. 2?
- If all the world is a stage, where is the audience sitting?

Finally, my own personal time honored truth still is, "I believe our lives would be a lot less stressful, if we all would lighten up, smile, be happy and don't sweat the little things."

Have a great day and enjoy your life.

Spending Some Time at God's House – October 12, 2001

To the editor:

I recently sent a letter to the editor commenting on some people playing golf on Sunday instead of going to church. I also gave an alternate prayer solution for Sunday golfers and even a comment on the proper dress attire for the church.

So what now? What did old Papa Joe do now? Well, several people complimented me on the article, but one individual remarked to me, "Joe, it is quite evident that you go to church every Sunday, but would you mind telling me why?"

Needless to say, I was quite surprised by such an unusual question, but I had to admit, a very interesting one. (Think about it a moment, have you ever been asked, "why do you go to church on Sunday?" When I recovered from my surprise I decided I would try to give him some kind of a reasonable answer and hopefully satisfy his curiosity.

Now, before your readers get the wrong impression; I am not reverting from my humorous (?) dissertations to become a religious contributor. I feel that I had started something with my last letter on "church going" and felt that I had better follow through and answer my friend's question with this, my last letter on religion.

I informed my curious friend that I didn't really feel I had to go to church on Sunday, and I probably wouldn't die and go to hell if I didn't go, (I think!!!) but it was something very satisfying and fulfilling for my spiritual needs, so I did it.

The reason I go to church is to visit and talk with God in His home.

My friend also surprised me with a second question, "What do you talk to God about?" At this point, I told him he was getting a little too personal, but after thinking it over for a little while, I decided to give him a "quickie" answer.

I told him when I go to church, I participate in all the activities, but I take sufficient time to express my deep thanks and appreciation to God for all the good and wonderful things He has given me and done for me, my entire life. (That's a long time!)

I also take the time to beg God's forgiveness for the "?" things I may have committed or done, and pray that He give me guidance and help me be a much better person the rest of my life. (That's why I go to church 15-20 minutes early each Sunday – so I'll have plenty of time to cover all my bases.)

So, dear pilgrims, what it all boils down to is regardless of why you or I go to church, the important thing is that we go. So, whatcha say next Sunday let's put on some nice decent looking clothes and go to church. Just don't forget to say an extra little prayer for ole Papa Joe. Peace!

Did you ever wonder why a lot of people leave church early before the services are over? The only explanation I can come up with is they must pray a lot faster that most of us!

If a Pig Loses its Voice, is it Disgruntled? – December 17, 2001

To the editor:

Like most people, I have always had a curiosity and have found that as I ramble on through life, I encounter a lot of "What, whys and ifs." Frequently, I never find an answer, but I continue to search.

As such, I would like to pass on to your readers some of life's philosophical conundrums that I have encountered and hopefully they can come up with some answers. Here are a few to get them started.

- If olive oil comes from olives, where does baby oil come from?
- When someone asks you "A penny for your thoughts," and you put your two cents in, what happens to the other penny?
- If a pig loses its voice, is it disgruntled?
- Do Lipton tea employees take coffee breaks?
- If Fed Ex and UPS were to merge, would they call it Fed UP?
- Do infants enjoy infancy as much as adults enjoy adultery?
- When cheese gets its picture taken, what does it say?
- Whatever happened to Preparations A through G?
- Why isn't 11 pronounced "onety one?"
- Why do they put pictures of criminals up in the post office? What are we supposed to do, write to them? Why don't they put their pictures on the postage stamps so the mail person could look for them while delivering the mail?

Finally, one thing that I have found to be true is that the holiday season is the most joyous time of the year. As such I would like to extend to you and your readers a wonderful happy holiday season.

More Truths of Life – November 21, 2001

To the editor:

I have been a "clipper" for most of my life. Over the years whenever I saw a humorous joke, quote, poem or anything that tickled my funny bone, I would clip it and save it.

Last night while going through some of my clippings, I found several more truths of life. I refer to them as "Things that took me 70-plus years to learn." I would like to share them and hope your readers enjoy them.

- Never take a sleeping pill and laxative on the same night.
- There is only one sure way to have a distant relative – lend him money.
- Anything you drop in the bathroom will land in the toilet.
- Never slap a man's face while he is chewing tobacco.
- It's too bad the only people who know how to run the country are too busy driving cabs or cutting hair.
- The more I learn, the more I realize how little I know.
- Never lick a steak knife.
- When I go to bed, I give my troubles to God – He will be up all night anyway.
- Driveways are longer when it snows.
- When everything is coming your way – you are probably going in the wrong direction.
- The dumbest question I ever heard … "where did you lose it?"
- I am a self-made man, but I think if I had to do it over again, I would call in someone else.

Finally, I would like to pass on my own personal philosophy of life – "Be happy, don't worry, enjoy life, keep a smile on your face, be kind to each other and especially, don't sweat the little things."

Don't Sweat Small Stuff – January 3, 2002

To the editor:

I just took my first walk of the new year. While out, I stopped at my friendly neighborhood grocery store to buy a Lotto ticket, so I can win millions of collars and retire – again!

One of the fellows at the store asked me "Joe, when are you going to write some more 'words of wisdom'?" I told him that as a matter of fact, during my walk, I was considering writing a letter to the editor about people who don't shovel the snow off their sidewalks. I'm in pretty good shape, so I don't mind walking in a little snow, but I was more concerned about some of the mail carriers.

Then I remembered one of my philosophies of life, "don't sweat the little things," so instead of complaining, I decided I would offer a few more of life's philosophical conundrums to start off the New Year.

- Why is there no jelly or beans in jelly beans?
- When you open a bag of cotton balls is the top one meant to be thrown away?
- Why isn't there a mouse flavored cat foot?
- Why do they lock gas station bathrooms? Are they afraid someone will clean them?
- Why don't they make airplanes out of the same material as that little black box?
- If a parsley farmer is sued, can they garnish his wages?
- Why do people who know the least, know it the loudest?
- If a turtle doesn't have a shell, is he homeless or naked?
- If the cops arrest a mime, do they tell him he has the right to become vocal?
- Should vegetarians eat animal cookies?
- If the funeral procession is at night, do folks drive with their headlights off?

Finally, now that I have you in a good mood (hopefully) – the next time it snows, how about going out and cleaning off your sidewalks/driveways so that nice mail carrier can deliver all those nice letters you were expecting – or maybe a few bills you weren't looking forward to receiving. I am sure they will really appreciate it!

Just remember, take it easy, don't hurt yourself and don't sweat the little things. Have a great 2002.

Murphy's Law is Just a Simple Creed – March 26, 2002

To the editor:

A few years ago, one of the topics of the time was "Murphy's Law." The dictionary defines it as "the principle that whatever can possibly go wrong will!" I recently had an experience that reminded me of this principle.

I have been playing the same six numbers in the Michigan Lottery hoping to "hit it big" and make the kids and grandkids rich, as well as several other charitable organizations, including my church.

A couple of weeks ago I decided not to play my usual numbers and put that extra buck or two in the Sunday collection basket. I rationalized that "one in the hand is worth two in the bush." Guess what? Yep, five of my six numbers were drawn that week! True, I would not have won a million or more, but enough that I could have put an extra few more bucks in the basket. Oh well, like they say, "there's always tomorrow!"

My unfortunate experience was an incentive to research the subject. I found that no one has been able to identify Murphy. I did read where some people thought h was an Air Force captain who put a rocket upside down in a space missile.

To really appreciate Murphy's Law, you first must answer a few questions:

Have you ever arrived at the railroad station just in time to see the last train depart? Are you always in the slow line rather than the one that moves faster? Does it rain just after you wash your car?

Now that you understand what Murphy's Law is all about, here's a couple of more.

Exciting sports event plays occur only when you go to the bathroom or to the fridge for a snack.

The "Consumer Report" on an item will come out a week after you've made your purchase. Corollaries: the one you bought will be rated "unacceptable" ; or the one you almost bought will be rated "best buy."

The one time you lean back to relax is the one time the boss walks through.

The one who snores falls asleep first.

Here's Murphy's Law on clothing shopping:

    1. If you like it, they don't have it in your size.

    2. If you like it and it's in your size, it doesn't fit anyway.

    3. If you like it and it fits, you can't afford it.

    4. If you like it, it fits and you can afford it, it falls apart the first time you wear it.

I think you can propound Murphy's Law of life is just 13 words: "You can't win, you can't break even, you can't even quit the game!"

So my advice to you is to consider "Papa Joe's laws" – keep a smile on your face, be happy, enjoy life and please, don't sweat the little things!

Contest Wants New Meanings for Those Old, Tired Words – April 26, 2002

To the editor:

One of the things I remember my mother teaching me, as a child, (boy, that was a long time ago!) was to try and learn a new word every day or so. She told me it would help improve my vocabulary and help me out later on in life.

Recently, one of my good friends informed me that The Washington Post had published a contest for readers in which they were asked to supply alternate meanings for various words. I was fortunate enough to see some of the winning entries, which I would like to pass on to your wordsmiths for their edification and consideration. Who knows, maybe we can all improve our vocabularies a little. Here goes:

- Lymph (v). To walk with a lisp
- Coffee (n). A person who is coughed upon.
- Flabbergasted (adj). Appalled over how much weight you have gained.
- Abdicate (v). To give up all hope of ever having a flat stomach.
- Bustard (n). A very rude metro-bus driver.

- Balderdash (n). A rapidly receding hairline.
- Circumvent (n). The opening in the front of boxer shorts.
- Negligent (adj). Describes a condition in which you absentmindedly answer the door in your nightie.

Finally, my personal contribution:

- Relativity (n). After three days, relatives, like fish, begin to smell and should be thrown out!

Only kidding! Just remember to be happy, enjoy life and keep a smile on your face. Be kind to teach other and don't sweat the little things.

Here are the Things Mother Taught – May 12, 2002

To the editor:

Last year on Mother's Day I submitted a list of time-honored truths about "real moms." Here's one your readers may remember: "Real moms have sticky floors, dirty ovens and happy kids."

Recently, while going through my old clippings, I found a list of several "Things my mother taught me." Needless to say I had a flashback to my own dear mother and some of the pearls of wisdom she used to give us kids. Maybe some of them will remind your readers of a few their mothers passed on to them while growing up.

- My mother taught me religion: You had better pray that the stuff you spilled will come out of the carpet."
- My mother taught me logic: "Because I said so, that's why!"
- My mother taught me control: "Keep laughing and I'll give you something to cry about."
- My mother taught me the science of osmosis: "Shut your mouth, and eat your supper."
- My mother taught me about being a contortionist: "Look at the back of your neck, it's filthy."
- My mother taught me about medical miracles: "If you fall off that thing and break your neck, don't come running to me."
- My mother taught me about the weather: "Your room looks like it was hit by a tornado."
- My mother taught me about straight talk: "If I told you once, I told you a million times, don't exaggerate."

Now that I have you thinking about mothers (that was my intention), I would like to remind you that Mother's Day is here, so please don't forget to give yours a big hug and kiss and tell her how much you love her. I'm sure that will make her very happy.

If you're lucky enough to still have a grandmother around, give her a big hug and kiss too. Remember, grandma is the one who lets you put your vegetables back in the pot if you don't want to eat them.

Happy Mother's Day.

Helpful Advice – June 4, 2002

To the editor:

Graduation time will soon be here so it's another opportunity for me to pass on some pearls of wisdom to the new graduates. As I mentioned one time, there are two kinds of education – the kind you get in school and the kind you get afterward.

The words of wisdom I am about to impart are not learned in school. Some of this wisdom is borrowed, some is stolen and some may even be original. I do know that the graduating seniors can save some years of trial, error and hard knocks by memorizing the lessons of life listed below:

- Life is not fair – get used to it.
- If you think your teacher is tough, wait until you get a boss.
- Television ruins more minds than drugs.
- Television is not real life. In real life, people actually have to leave the coffee shop and go to jobs.
- If you mess up, it's not your parents' fault. So don't whine about your mistakes, learn from them.
- Life is so much simpler when you tell the truth.

- Sometimes there is more to gain in being wrong than right.
- Be nice to nerds. Chances are you'll end up working for one.
- Before you were born, your parents weren't as boring as they are now. They go that way from paying your bills, cooking your meals, cleaning your clothes and listening to how cool you are. So before you save the rain forest from the parasites of your parents' generation, try delousing the closet in your own room.
- If you don't do anything else in life, love someone and let someone love you.

One final comment. I am finding out that as I age, I am learning more and more – now my problem is trying to remember it!

Congratulations, good luck and lots of success to all the high school graduates!

Celebrate Fathers – June 13, 2002

To the editor:

On Mother's Day I submitted a list of things my mother taught me. I received many favorable comments from my friends who told me of several other "things" their mothers had taught them as kids. I guess all mothers are dispensers of good, wise and meaningful wisdom!

The other day I got to thinking about "things my father taught me" and for some reason or other, it just wasn't the same. I guess a mother's teachings are very special and can't be duplicated.

Fathers are special in their own way. So, what is a father? Ask a hundred people and you'll probably get a hundred answers. Sometime ago, I saw a list of definitions of what a father was. Maybe your readers would like to add to this list. A father is a person:

- Who can fish a skate key out of a heating vent, fix a flat tire and make pancakes better than mom.
- Who makes mom giggle, pop corn and get messages to the tooth fairy.
- Who knows what you're thinking before you think it.
- Who knows how to talk mom into letting the latest stray spend the night in the basement.
- Who makes you the tallest person in the world when he sits you on his shoulders.
- Who likes to pass on pearls of wisdom he picked up at work. Here's a few examples:
- Never squat with your spurs on.
- Never ask a barber if you need a haircut.
- You don't have to go to medical school to learn that lending money to your relatives can cause amnesia.
- Never pass up the opportunity to use the bathroom. It may be your last chance for a long time.
- A real father only needs two tools – WD 40 and duct tape. If it doesn't move and it should, use WD 40. If it moves and it shouldn't use the tape.

So, to all the children out there, Father's Day will soon be here and regardless of what you call him, pop, dad, pa, pap, father or whatever, give him a big hug and tell him you love and appreciate him. Who knows, he may even take you out to dinner.

Happy Father's Day!

Have a Good 4th – June 28, 2002

To the editor:

July 4, 1776, the adoption of the Declaration of Independence. (Actually, I don't think all the signatures were affixed until January 1777, but who's counting?)

I remember with nostalgia the good old-fashioned Fourth of July. The reasonably quiet neighborhoods and the noisy firecracker purchased at the corner drugstore. The racket only lasted a day or two!

Unfortunately there were casualties and these surely justified the reasonably safe and sane July fourths we have today.

Today we have very few parades or speeches, but we do have very elaborate fireworks displays that everyone enjoys safely. One thing that hasn't changed is that the average American is very proud and has confidence in the United States, still the best country in the world.

Despite our heritage and all of its redeeming privileges, Americans still have a few idiosyncrasies. Here are a few examples.

Only in America:

- Do people order double cheeseburgers, a large order of fries and a diet Coke.
- Do we buy hot dogs in packages of 10 and buns in packages of eight.
- Do we leave cars worth thousands of dollars in the driveway and keep useless junk in the garage.
- Do banks leave both doors open and then chain the pens to the counters.
- Do drugstores make the sick customers walk all the way to the back of the store to get their prescriptions.
- Do we use answering machines to screen calls, and then, have call waiting so we don't miss a call from someone we didn't want to talk to in the first place.

One final comment for your consideration: If you do hit the highways this Fourth of July, please remember this, "He goes forth with a fifth on the Fourth, may not come forth on the fifth."

So, God bless America, buckle up, drive sober and sane, safely, and have a happy Fourth of July.

A Few Thoughts on a Treasured Subject – July 26, 2002

To the editor:

Recently I was having a hamburger and iced tea at one of my favorite bistros when I was hassled by a couple of old friends. They mentioned that I had written many letters to the editor on a wide variety of subjects but I had never written anything about their favorite subject – beer.

Since I want to keep my friends happy, I researched the subject and came up with some quotes on the subject by several famous people. So here's to the boys at the "Big B."

"I feel sorry for people who don't drink. When they wake up in the morning, that's as good as they're going to feel all day." – Frank Sinatra

"Beer is proof that God loves us and wants us to be happy." – Benjamin Franklin

"24 hours in a day. 24 beers in a case, coincidence?" – Stephen Wright

"Sometimes when I reflect back on all the beer I drink I feel ashamed. Then I look into the glass and think about the workers in the brewery and all of their hopes and dreams. If I didn't drink this beer they might be out of work and their dreams would be shattered. Then I say to myself, 'It is better that I drink this beer and let their dreams come true than be worried selfish and worry about my liver.'" – Jack Hardy

"When I read about the evils of drinking, I gave up reading." – Henny Youngman

"A woman drove me to drink and I didn't even have the decency to thank her." – W.C. Fields

Seriously folks, this is only humor and I hope you take it as such and with a grain of salt. If you put salt in your beer, please make sure it's non-alcoholic beer.

Kids Write the Darnedest Things – December 6, 2002

To the editor:

Several years ago, there was a TV show entitled "Kids Say the Darnedest Things." The children on the show were rather uninhibited and mostly answered the questions with the first thing that popped into their minds. Needless to say, there was a lot of good, clean humor on the program.

I was reminded of this show recently when my school teacher daughter, Sally, sent me some actual test answers from the various schools in the Huntsville, Ala., metropolitan area. I would like to pass on a few of these "jewels," which I am sure will bring a smile to your readers' faces.

Q.   Name the four seasons.
A.   Salt, pepper, mustard and vinegar.

Q.   How is dew formed?
A.   The sun shines down on the leaves and makes them perspire.
Q.   Name a major disease associated with cigarettes.
A.   Premature death.
Q.   What happens to your body as you age?
A.   When you get old, so do your bowels, and you get intercontinental.
Q.   How can you delay milk turning sour?
A.   Keep it in the cow.
Q.   What is the fibula?
A.   A small lie.
Q.   What is a terminal illness?
A.   When you get sick at the airport.
Q.   What does the word "benign" mean?
A.   Benign is what you will be after you be eight.

Out of the mouths of babes, eh? So, whatcha think? Pretend you're the teacher – what kind of grade would you give them? Personally, I think we have to give credit to those creative minds, and I believe they all deserve A's.

I am also confident they'll all grow up to be good, bright and highly intelligent citizens. One thing's for sure, I bet they won't have to go to medical school to learn that lending money to relatives can cause amnesia.

P.S. Did you give someone a hug today?

Really Give Thanks on Thanksgiving Day – November 19, 2002

To the editor:

Thanksgiving Day is the day we give thanks for all the good things God has bestowed upon us. It is also the day that most of us indulge ourselves with that gigantic, delicious dinner – turkey with all the trimmings.

Personally, I am thankful that as I continue to mature, I am learning to be happy, enjoy life, think positive, live for today, and not sweat the little things – especially things that I have no control over; like my wrinkles, gray hair (at least I have some hair!) The bald spot on the back of my head (I can't see it anyway!) and the belt that bears a few marks of an expanding waist line (does leather shrink?)

I would like to thank all of you for the friendship you have shared with me over the years, and wish you peace and happiness and lots and lots of good luck.

I hope you enjoy your Thanksgiving dinner and remember what I said about not sweating the little things. If you should eat a little too much and start to feel a little drowsy – not to worry, take a nap and relax. You have a long weekend to clean up and do the dishes! Happy Thanksgiving.

Seatbelt Would have saved Daughter's Life – December 23, 2002

To the editor:

We have all been hearing and reading about the recent publicity going on to get people to wear their seat belts. "Ticket if you don't click it." Sounds kind of funny doesn't it? Believe me, it isn't! It can be the most important thing you ever do in your life. It could be the difference between your life or your death.

Let me tell you a little story. Twenty-five years ago, two of my daughters were visiting my wife and me for a long weekend. Since the girls hadn't seen each other for awhile, they decided to go shopping and run around town. As they left the house, they were laughing and giggling as young sisters will do. In fact, we were all laughing and happy.

When the dinner hour approached and the girls were not home, we began to worry. Then the phone rang, and we thought they were "reporting in." Instead it was the police informing us the girls had been in an accident and we should come to the hospital immediately.

When we got there, a doctor informed us that one of our daughters was okay, but the other one, a bride of only several weeks, was dead.

They were only a few blocks away and on their way home, when the car hit the curb and rolled over. How could this terrible thing happen when they were only driving 25-30 mph down a one-way street?

Why? Because the girls were not wearing their seat belts. On their way home, they had stopped at a store to buy snacks for the evening, and in the jubilance, they forgot to put on their seat belts. If they had, I would still have three daughters today instead of two. The daughter killed was once Midland's Miss United Fund. A wonderful and beautiful lady.

Now do you understand why I am a firm believer and endorse the "Ticket if you don't click it" program? It's not the ticket you should worry about, though, it's the life you could save or lose – yours!

So, dear friends, instead of thinking up a lot of reasons not to buckle up – because "it won't or can't happen to me" – believe me, it can and does happen.

So, whatever the slogan may be, "ticket if you don't click it" or any other, just do it – buckle up! I'm sure you'll feel more secure and safe and I'm positive it will bring a smile to Susie's face, wherever she may be.

Thank you and safe driving.

Ponderings – August 8, 2002

To the editor:

Last year I submitted what I called at the time some philosophical conundrums. Since then some of my friends (yes, I still have a few!) started sending me more. Some were referred to as ponderings, just wondering and a few other names. Regardless of what they are called, I would like to pass them on to your readers for their enjoyment.

- If people from Poland are called Poles, why aren't people from Holland called Holes?
- Why do croutons come in airtight packages? It's just stale bread to begin with.
- If you mixed vodka and orange juice with milk of magnesia, would you get a Phillips screwdriver?
- When dog food is new and improved tasting, who tests it?
- Why doesn't the glue stick to the inside of the bottle?
- How does the guy who drives the snowplow get to work?
- If four out of five people suffer from diarrhea, does that mean that one enjoys it?
- We feed babies with tiny little spoons and forks. Wonder what Chinese mothers use. Toothpicks?
- What do chickens think we taste like?
- Why are cigarettes sold at gas stations where smoking is prohibited?
- Why don't sheep shrink when it rains?
- Why didn't Noah swat those two mosquitoes on the ark?

Finally, I would like to pass on one final comment and bit of advice a friend sent to me – "If a person calls you a donkey or an ass, you better buy a saddle."

Personally, I think that if you're happy, enjoy life, don't worry, keep a smile on your face and are kind to each other, none of us will need a saddle!

Take the Time to Give Someone a Hug Today – November 10, 2002

To the editor:

The other day I found a small book that my youngest daughter Sara had given to me almost 20 years ago. The title of the book is "The Hug Therapy Book," and inside the front cover was the inscription "To my best little hugger – Papa Joe."

Boy, that sure brought back a flood of good memories and happy thoughts. I never was much of a hugger before then, but I have been trying to make up for it ever since.

There are several recommended types and methods of hugs, but I have always tried to do it the natural way – let it happen at any time or any place.

So very much is written about hugging and even though it is free, very few people ever take advantage of it. I recently read where hugging is not only nice, and needed, but scientific research supports the theory that stimulation by touch is absolutely necessary for our physical as well as our emotional well being.

Hugging feels good, builds self esteem, eases tensions, makes happy days happier, and it especially keeps our arm and shoulder muscles in good condition!

I saw a quote at a nursing home the other day which I would like to pass on to your readers. "Hugging is nothing less than a miracle drug. Hugging is all natural. It is organic, naturally sweet, no artificial ingredients, non polluting, environmentally friendly, and 100 percent wholesome."

So dear friends Ii am advocating and promoting hugging – starting right now! As you read this, who is the closest person near you? Now go to that person, slim or tall, big or small, and say, "I need a hug!" Surprise! Now didn't that feel nice and give you a warm fuzzy feeling?

Just remember, always ask first for your hug! And, when you hug naturally do it within the guidelines of proper propriety! Also, hubs cannot be bought, begged, borrowed or stolen because it is of no value to anyone until it is given away. So give a hug away as soon as you can – you will feel good, as will the recipient.

One last comment. If you see old Papa Joe out there and about and you need or would like a hug, I am more than happy to oblige. I can always use an extra hug or two myself.

What You Need to Know About Grandchildren – January 7, 2003

To the editor:

I was very fortunate this holiday season to be able to spend a few days with some of my grandchildren. On my return home, some of my friends inquired as to how my visit went. Invariably the talk turned to grandchildren and how they have a tendency to cause pandemonium and disrupt the normal flow of the household activities.

As we reminisced, we came to the realization that despite all of their little idiosyncrasies, we do learn a lot of things from our children. I would like to pass on a few of these "gems" to the younger moms and dads who are just starting to raise their families.

The most important thing you will learn is "patience" – lots and lots of patience! As I have made my way through life, here are a few things I have learned from my children and grandchildren.

- A 3-year-old's voice is louder than 200 adults in a crowded restaurant.
- A king-size waterbed holds enough water to fill a 2000 square foot ranch house ¼ inch deep.
- You should not throw baseballs up when the ceiling fan is on. When using the ceiling fan as a bat, you have to throw the balls up a few times before you get a hit. A ceiling fan can hit a baseball a long way!
- The glass in windows (even double pan) doesn't stop a baseball hit by a ceiling fan.
- Brake fluid mixed with Clorox makes smoke – and lots of it.
- If you hook a dog leash over a ceiling fan, the motor is not strong enough to rotate a 42-pound boy wearing Batman underwear and a Superman cape.
- Certain LEGOs will pass through the digestive tract of a 4-year-old.
- When you hear the toilet flush and the words "uh-oh," it's already too late.

With those thoughts in mind, the best advice I can give young moms and dads is to keep a close eye on those little ragamuffins running around the house. Especially the ones with sweet, smiling and innocent faces. The little devils! Another great idea is to give them a hug and kiss – that will distract them for a few minutes.

Some "Golden Year" Discoveries – February 10, 2003

To the editor:

Most of my friends and I have reached what they call the Golden Years. My definition is not worthy to be published in this letter, but the next time you see me out in public, stop me and I'll whisper the definition of Golden Years in your ear.

I've been called many things, including senior citizen and dirty ole man (I prefer sexy senior citizen!). The dictionary defines mature, which is how I describe myself, as having reached a full state of natural development or of being ripe like a peach or tomato. Would someone please explain that to me?

Anyway, now that I'm more mature (but refuse to grow up) here are some of the things I have discovered in my golden years.

I started out with nothing and I still have most of it.

My wild oats have turned into prunes and bran.

I finally got my head together; now my body is falling apart.

All reports are now in; life is now officially unfair.

If all is not lost, where is it?

It is easier to get older than it is to get wiser.

Some day you're dog; some days you're the hydrant.

I wish the buck stopped here; I sure could use a few.

Kids in the back seat cause accidents. Accidents in the back seat cause kids.

It's hard to make a comeback when you haven't been anywhere.

The only time the world beats a path to your door is when you're in the bathroom.

If God wanted me to touch my toes, he would have put them on my knees.

These days I spend a lot of time thinking about the hereafter … I go somewhere to get something and then wonder what I'm here after.

Ponderings – March 4, 2003

To the editor:

As I continue to write letters to the editor, I have accumulated a following of well wishers who frequently ask, "have you heard the one about the …" As such, I have started accumulating a collection of wonderings or ponderings.

Whatever you call them, I think they are humorous and I would be remiss if I didn't pass some of them on to readers for their enjoyment.

- If a man is standing in the middle of a forest speaking and there is no woman around to hear him – is he still wrong?
- The main reason Santa is so jolly is because he knows where all the bad girls live.
- Where do the forest rangers go to get away from it all?
- How do they get the deer to cross at that yellow road sign?
- Is it true that cannibals don't eat clowns because they taste funny?
- What was the best thing before sliced bread?
- Why is it called tourist season if we can't shoot at them?
- Why is the alphabet in that order? Is it because of that song?
- If the "black box" flight recorder is never damaged during a plane crash, why isn't the whole airplane made out of that stuff?

Finally, a piece of Papa Joe's wisdom on life. I sincerely believe that the key to happiness and an enjoyable life is to have a positive attitude and a good sense of humor. Keep on smiling and don't sweat the little things.

Tips for Dealing with Shopping – April 10, 2003

To the editor:

The other day our luncheon society got together for our monthly sojourn. The meeting consisted of eating a nice meal to give us strength in our journey through life and a B.S. (better solutions) session in solving some of the world's worst problems.

As we were about to adjourn, I mentioned I had a little shopping to do. Immediately our meeting was back in session again, as it seems a lot of the fellas don't like shopping.

They said they didn't mind shopping too much in the earlier years of their marriage because it was sort of a "lovey dovey" thing to do with their beautiful brides. Besides, they quickly learned that if they said no to shopping, these nice young ladies would start crying and saying, "you don't love me anymore!" Then they would feel worse than a kid having to take a bath on Saturday night.

As time went on, they found out that shopping was really boring. Then they decided if they were going to entertain themselves as their spouses shopped, they would have to come up with some ingenious plans or ideas to amuse themselves.

They came up with several suggestions that I would like to pass on to readers. Give them a try and let me know how you make out. Here goes:

- Set the alarm clocks in housewares to go off at five minute intervals.
- Go to the service desk and ask to put a bag of M&M's on layaway.
- When a clerk asks if he or she can help you, begin to cry and ask "why can't you people just leave me alone?"
- Look directly into the security camera and use it as a mirror to pick your nose.
- Hide in a clothing rack and when people browse through say, "pick me! Pick me!"

Just remember to keep a positive attitude, have a good sense of humor and keep a smile on your face. Also, don't sweat the little things – which also means "no shoplifting."

On Being Nice to Your Children – May 28, 2003

To the editor:

Fifty plus years ago on a business trip to Buffalo, N.Y., I met a beautiful, young and talented lady named Marjorie Rose Miller. I eventually married her and moved her to Midland where we lived and raised a family of four beautiful children.

Marjorie was a registered nurse and worked for several years at the Midland hospital – in between having and raising children.

Recently, I found in one of her drawers, a list of humorous medical definitions which I think your readers will enjoy. Here are a few of them for their entertainment:

- Barium: what you do if they die.
- Cat scan: search for a kitty.
- Cauterize: made eye contact with her.
- Colic: a sheep dog.
- Labor pain: getting hurt at work
- Nitrates: cheaper than day rates.
- Outpatients: a person who has fainted.

One word of advice I would like to pass on to you elderly parents – "always be nice to your children because they will be the ones to choose your nursing home."

Be kind to each other, keep a smile on your face, be happy, enjoy life and don't sweat the little things.

And Don't Forget Father's Day – June 13, 2003

To the editor:

As we all know mothers get a lot of praise throughout the year, especially on Mother's day. Flowers, candy, presents, taken out to dinner, given lots of hugs and kisses and they deserve all of it – and more.

But poor old Dad! Too often we take him for granted and forget that he is the jack of all trades that helps keep the family rolling along. He is very special, especially as a dispenser of good, wise and meaningful wisdom.

We all have our own opinion of what our fathers mean to us individually. However, I have come up with a list of definitions of what I think a father is – would you like to add to this list? A father is:

- A person who can tell what birds are saying, why God made ants and how spiders can crawl upside down.
- A person who yells at you when you slam the door but listens patiently while you explain why the principal called.
- The reason you pull weeds, mow the lawn, wash the dog and do not put gum in the car ashtray.
- A person who will not scold you for digging holes in the back yard if you find some good fishing worms.
- A person who can sleep the night before his little girl's first date, and then brings her a rose from work to celebrate the event.
- A person who knows that loving his children is his favorite form of prayer.

So, to all you folks out there who have a father, dad, pop, pa, papa, or whatever you call him, make sure you give him a big hug for Father's Day. You ladies, young and more mature (never old!) also give him a great big smoochie kiss. Also tell him how much you love and appreciate him and he might take you out for a Big Mac – including fries (freedom fries that is).

Happy Father's Day to all you dads out there – young and ole (yep, dads can be called old instead of more mature).

Life's Advice – June 6, 2003

To the editor:

Recently, my daughter Sally, the school teacher, studying in her spare time, (what is spare time?) graduated cum laude with a master's of education degree in mathematics. Needless to say, I am very proud of her and the other graduates who have put forth a lot of effort to achieve their accomplishments.

As you can imagine, I have "graduation" on my mind right now. As such, I think this is an appropriate time to pass on some words of wisdom to the high school graduates.

First of all, I would like to extend my personal congratulations to all graduates and wish them lots of luck and success in their future endeavors in life.

I know they have learned many things in school, but just like "after school hours" there are other things in life that can't be learned in school. As such I would like to pass on a few tidbits I have learned in my journey through life. Welcome aboard.

- You will not make 40k/year right out of high school. You won't be a vice president with a car phone until you earn both.
- Persistence will get you almost anything eventually.
- Baby kittens don't begin to open their eyes for six weeks after birth. Some people take about 26 years.
- Flipping burgers is not beneath your dignity. Your grandparents had a different word for it – they called it opportunity.
- Life is not divided into semesters. You don't get summers off and very few employers are interested in helping you find yourself.
- Life is full of surprises. Just say "never" and you'll see.
- The world would run a lot smoother if more men knew how to dance.

- Live by what you trust, not by what you fear.
- Character counts. Family matters.
- Forgive yourself, your friends and your enemies. You're all only human.
- Mother's always know best, but sometimes fathers know too.
- Eating out with small children isn't worth it – even if someone else is buying.

My final bit of advice is to not take yourself too seriously, have a positive attitude, a good sense of humor and don't sweat the little things.

There are Always Unanswered Questions – July 22, 2003

To the editor:

My 14-year-old granddaughter from Texas is visiting me and, needless to say, it is quite an experience for an old man used to living alone. I have been trying to impress her with my philosophies of life and one thing I have tried to convince her of is that the older I get the wiser I get.

I was even convincing myself until my son-in-law sent me a list of questions, but no answers. After looking over the questions, I don't feel so wise anymore. Anyway, I thought I would pass on a few of these "innovative" questions to see if they can titillate your readers' consciousness as they did mine. Here goes:

- Why is the third hand on the watch called the second hand?
- If a word is misspelled in the dictionary, then how would we know?
- If Webster wrote the first dictionary, where did he find the words?
- Why do we say something is out of whack? What is a whack?
- Why do "fat chance" and "slim chance" mean the same thing?
- Why do we sing "take me out to the ball game" when we are already there?
- Why are a "wise man" and a "wise guy" opposites?
- If work is so terrific, why do they have to pay you to do it?
- If all the world is a stage, where's the audience sitting?
- Why do we wash towels? Aren't we clean when we use them?
- Why do they call it a TV set when we only have one?

One thing my granddaughter observed during our tour of Midland was, "Papa Joe, you sure do know a lot of people?" Finally, here was my chance to impress her and give her a few of my philosophies of life: "Be patient, tolerant, understanding, compassionate, keep a smile on your face, and be kind to each other." Also give someone a big hug today and you will have another friend!

I don't know if I impressed Kaitlyn Rose or not, but she had a big smile on her face as she boarded the plane for her flight back to Texas.

Golf's in Full Swing – July 2, 2003

To the editor:

Although golf season has been here for a couple of months, it has only been a few weeks that it has been warm enough so we can play in our shorts instead of our long johns. However, with my long johns no one laughed at my knobby knees!

Since we are now in full swing (no pun intended), I would like to pass on some golf quotes by some famous people. There are also a few quotes by some of my not-so-famous friends and their last names have been eliminated to protect the innocent.

- I know I am getting better at golf because I am hitting few spectators. Gerald Ford
- It took me 17 years to get three thousand hits in baseball. I did it in one afternoon on the golf course. Hank Aaron
- My handicap? Woods and irons. Jack W.
- The only time my prayers are not answered is on the golf course. Billy Graham

- Golf is a game in which you yell "fore", shoot six, and write down five. Paul Harvey
- My body is here but my mind has already teed off. Roger J.
- Give me golf clubs, fresh air, and a beautiful partner, and you can keep the clubs and the fresh air. Jack Benny
- If I hit it right, it's a slice. If I hit it left, it's a hook. If I hit it straight, it's a miracle. Chuck L.
- It's good sportsmanship to not pick up lost golf balls while they are still rolling. Mark Twain
- The difference in golf and government is that in golf you can't improve your lie. Elmer F.
- If you think it's hard to meet new people, try picking up the wrong golf ball. Jack Lemmon
- Golf is a game invented by the same people who think music comes out of a bagpipe. Andy D.

Happy golfing or whatever they say. Enjoy yourself and don't sweat the little things. However, since there are no gimmies in golf, you may have to sweat a few "little things" such as those 12 to 18 inch putts! Have a great day.

A Warning – August 22, 2003

To the editor:

"Don't drink and Drive" and "Drunk Drivers Go To Jail." How many times have we read or heard these warnings?

Regardless of the warnings some people still have a tendency to partake of the juice of the grape a little too abundantly or imbibe too heavily on the joy juice of the barley and hops. This is normally done at the local neighborhood "Cheers," where everyone knows you by name!

When all the words of wisdom have been expounded and the world's problems have been solved (or the missus calls and tells the bartender to "kick out that drunken bum and send him home") it's time to go. One more for the road and a final trip to the john and our friend is on his way.

Now, instead of taking a slow leisurely drive home our friend thinks he's at the Indianapolis 500 Speedway and varoom, varoom, and away he goes!! Little does he realize that he is only speeding to his doom – death, a helluva lecture from his better half, or a small piece of paper from one of those gentlemen in a blue suit wearing a silver badge!

If our friend is lucky he'll get one of the last two options, and neither one is a piece of cake!!! Should he get stopped by the nice gentleman with the silver badge, I would like to give him a little free advice. Contrary to what you might like to say to him I would suggest you not even consider saying any of the following things to that nice man with the badge:

- Sorry, Officer, I didn't realize my radar detector wasn't plugged in.
- Hey!, you must have been doing about 125 mph to keep up with me. Good job!
- I can't reach my license unless you hold my beer.
- I thought you had to be in relatively good physical condition to be a police officer.
- You're not going to check the trunk are you?
- I pay your salary you know!
- Do you know why you pulled me over? Okay, just so one of us does.
- I was trying to keep up with traffic. Yes, I know there are no other cars around. That's how far ahead of me they are.
- When the officer says, "Gee son, your eyes look red, have you been drinking?" you probably shouldn't respond with, "Gee officer, your eyes look glazed, have you been eating donuts?"

Finally, one bit of advice I would like to give to our friend if he should decide to go out drinking again. Get yourself a designated driver but not a good friend. You wouldn't want a good friend to see you make an ass out of yourself from drinking too much would you?? Only you can answer that question!!!

Children Offer Look at the Meaning of Love – September 22, 2003

To the editor:

School Days! School Days! Good old golden rule days. All of the children are back in school again. Do you miss them yet moms – especially the little ones? I'll give you another week or two and then ask!

Last year, I shared some questions that were asked of young children and the answers they gave. An example: Q.: How can you keep milk from turning sour? A: Keep it in the cow.

Clever, aren't they? Did you ever wonder what a group of first- and second-graders would answer when asked, "What does love mean?" A group of teachers recently posed this question and the answers they got back were broader and deeper than anyone could imagine. Take a look:

- Love is when a girl puts on perfume and a boy puts on shaving cologne and they go out and smell each other."
- Love is when you go out to eat and give somebody most of your French fries without making them give you any of theirs.
- Love is what makes you smile when you're tired.
- Love is when you tell a guy you like his shirt and he wears it every day.
- Love is like a little old woman and a little old man who are still friends even after they know each other so well.
- Love is when mommy gives daddy the best piece of chicken.
- Love is when your puppy licks your face even after you left him alone a day.
- When you love somebody, your eyelashes go up and down and little stars come out of you.

Like they say, it takes all kinds but "love really does make the world go around." Parents, if you have a lot of tension and a headache, do what it says on the aspirin bottle – take two aspirin and keep away from the kids. Only kidding! If you do get a little uptight or a little stressed out, give those little darlings a big hug and kiss and you'll both feel like a million bucks.

Have a great day and don't sweat the little things. No, not the kids – those little things in your lives!

More "Wisdom" – October 20, 2003

To the editor:

In the past, I have shared all types of "words of wisdom" from kids to the elderly (never old!) and everything in between. However, I don't think I have ever passed on any good old country wisdom.

So, let's see what those country folks can pass on to enlighten our day. Some of it may not make much sense to some of us city slickers, but believe me, these country folks know what they are talking about. Most importantly, they grow, raise and supply most of the food that goes on our dinner tables so the least we can do is be thankful to them and listen to their philosophies of life. Right? Right!

- Don't name a pig you plan to eat.
- Life is simpler when you plow around the stump.
- A bumblebee is a lot faster than a John Deere tractor.
- The trouble with a milk cow is she won't stay milked.
- Don't skinny dip in a pond where there are snapping turtles.
- Don't corner something meaner than you.
- You can catch more flies with honey than vinegar, assuming you want to catch flies.

Country folks seem like a nice group of relaxed, fun-loving and easygoing people, don't they? It's because they're happy, enjoy life, take one day at a time and they don't sweat the little things. And they always have smiles on their faces.

Readers Share Why They are Thankful – November 27, 2003

To the editor:

Thanksgiving Day is the day we give thanks for all the good things of the past year. Why do we only pick one day out of the 365 days a year to give thanks? Our lives are so full of good things, we should have our own little Thanksgiving every day – but without the turkey!

Each of us have our own things to be thankful for, but this Thanksgiving day when I bow my head at the dining room table, here's a few things I'll give thanks for.

- First and foremost, my wonderful family and our good health.
- I am especially thankful that my children and grandchildren have never, even for one day, awakened to the uncertain dawn that the children of many countries endure every day.
- A soft touch or hug from my grandchildren. A kiss on the cheek is even better and is certain to make my heart flutter.
- I have lived with the realization that hoping for something will have no effect on whether or not it will actually happen. I have found a prayer to be much more effective.
- I used to be thankful when I got a birdie playing golf – now I'm thankful for a par or two.
- I'm thankful for a warm bed on a cold night and a cool car on a hot day.
- Beautiful warm and sunny days.
- I am truly thankful that as I am aging I am learning to be happier, enjoying life more and "not sweating the little things", especially things that I don't have any control over – like wrinkles, gray hair, bald spots and an expanding waistline. (Ho! Ho! Ho!)

See, we all have so much to be thankful for – a beautiful country to live in, warm homes, good food and most of all, the love of our family and friends. Thanks to all of you for the friendship you have shared with my family over the years. I wish you peace and happiness. Have a great holiday feast with your family.

One final wish to you all: May your stuffing be tasty, may your turkey be plump. May your potatoes 'n' gravy have nary a lump. May your yams be delicious, may your pies take the prize. May your Thanksgiving dinner stay off of your thighs.

Where's the Family? – November 28, 2003

To the editor:

The other day, as I was visiting my wife in the nursing home, I had a sudden feeling of mixed emotions. Happy that I am able to visit her three times daily, but sad to notice that many of the other residents seldom have visitors.

Quite often when visiting my wife, I take the time to stop and visit several of those dear, sweet and lonely ladies. Fortunately, for an unfortunate, I have come to know more happiness than ever in my life.

I have learned that happiness can be seeing an older woman smile as I approach her and she extends her frail little arms to give me a greeting of appreciation and gratitude for taking the time to stop and visit with her. Where is her family?

Happiness is also hearing her feeble attempt to communicate with me and show her gratitude for the happiness I bring into her little world and lonely life. Where is her family?

Happiness is putting my arms around that frail and feeble body and gently patting her on the shoulder and then giving her a gentle kiss on the cheek. Then, as I gently hold her hand, she looks at me with kindness and gratitude for taking the time to visit her. Where is her family?

Ultimate happiness is when I get ready to depart, she gently and feebly raises my hand to her lips and kisses it in appreciation and gratitude and then she whispers to me in her soft and gentle voice, "Thank you for coming to see me – please come and visit me again." Where is her family?

What a shame her family and friend(s)? are too busy to visit and spend a little time with a loved one. If they only knew what they were missing! They could be receiving the love and gratitude of someone who only has a limited amount of time left. Where is her family?

Unfortunately, there are some residents who may not be able to see you or touch you or maybe they still need your visits and the love that comes with them – and lots of it. They need to be touched with love.

When I visit my dear, sweet wife, she doesn't know I am there, but she does know I'm there! Contradictory? Certainly not! When I visit her and gently hold her hand and squeeze it and whisper, "I love you," she gently but firmly squeezes my hand. Do you think she knows I am there or not?

So dear friends, I would like to make a plea to you today. If you have a loved one or friend in a nursing home, take the time to visit them and help brighten their day. I am positive you will get as much out of the visit as they will. Watch their eyes light up and the smile on their faces when you go to visit them. What a sight to behold.

Too Old for "Cool" – December 14, 2003

To the editor:

As many of my fellow "seniors" know, quite often some of our fellow patriots wear clothes, styles or combinations of both that cause the younger generation (smart alecks) to laugh or make fun of us. If they only knew we are having the same derogatory thoughts about their clothing, hair-dos and body piercings. The only trouble is, some seniors are trying to emulate the younger folks' lifestyles because they want to be "cool." Ha!

Since I have been exposed to many senior citizens, I have carefully observed their clothing customs and orientations, and have recorded some "Senior Fashion Tips," which I would like to pass on to them.

Regardless of what you seniors may have seen on the streets, these are the fashion tips you should observe. The following combinations do not go together!

- A nose ring and bifocals
- Spiked hair and bald spots
- Miniskirts and support hose
- Ankle bracelets and corn pads
- Speedos and cellulite
- A belly button ring and a gallbladder surgery scar
- Unbuttoned disco shirts and a heart monitor
- Midriff shirts and a midriff bulge
- Bikinis and liver spots
- Short shorts and varicose veins
- In-line skates and a walker

So, fellow seniors, let's forget the "cool" bit – you're too old and cold to be cool. But, otherwise, you're looking good so hang in there!

Why Not Give the Gift of Love this Christmas Season? – December 22, 2003

To the editor:

I heard on the radio the other day where parents will be spending an average of $150 a child on Christmas gifts. (That doesn't include gifts from Grandma and Grandpa!) Aren't things getting a little out of hand by showering our children and grandchildren with all those earthly things?

We all enjoy the holiday season and receiving gifts is wonderful, but maybe we should concentrate a little more on the giving, sharing, and love aspects of Christmas.

I believe we should spend more time on teaching our children and grandchildren the values of traditions so they can learn from the past and plan for the future. Don't just tell your children the values of the past by word, but more importantly by deed.

Children learn from what they see and hear: honesty, respect, charity, safety and caring for those less fortunate. Teach your child to be a giver. (Remember – "Tis better to give than receive"). Why not talk your child into taking one of his/her gifts and giving it to some less fortunate child who won't be having a $150 Christmas?

We can't forget adults either – we have to learn and live by the rules or guidelines of giving. We don't have to give monetary or earthly gifts, but there is always the gift of love.

Last year I received a Christmas card that's message was: "Help us Lord to remember what this season is for. Get us past all the glitter; let our hearts search for more. You have blessed us so richly, more than we're worthy of, but help us Lord to remember what's important. Love."

So, why not give the gift of love for Christmas? I have a particularly brilliant idea for some people to consider. Do you have a loved one or friend in a nursing home? Why not take a few minutes of your time during this holiday season to visit them and help brighten their lives? Give them a Christmas gift of love and while you're at it, throw in a few free hugs!

My wife and I would like to wish you a very special and happy, healthy holiday season and may God always keep you in the palm of His hand.

Getting a Few Smiles – January 21, 2004

To the editor:

Things have been a little hectic lately due to the holidays and anonymous letter writers, so I thought I would try to dispense a little levity and try to get a few smiles and laughs. I have accumulated a few "puns and truisms" which I would like to pass on to readers for their enjoyment. Here goes:

ADULT: A person who has stopped growing at both ends and is now growing in the middle.

BEAUTY PARLOR: A place where people can curl up and dye.

CANNIBAL: Someone who is fed up with people.

CHICKENS: The only animals you eat before they are born and after they are dead.

DUST: Mud with the juice squeezed out.

EGOTIST: Someone who is usually me-deep in conversation.

GOSSIP: A person who will never tell a lie if the truth will do more damage.

HANDKERCHIEF: Cold storage

INFLATION: Cutting money in half without damaging the paper.

MYTH: A female moth.

MOSQUITO: An insect that makes you like flies better.

RAISIN: A sunburned grape.

SECRET: Something you tell to one person at a time.

SKELETON: A bunch of bones with the person scraped off.

TOOTHACHE: The pain that drives you to extraction.

TOMORROW: One of the greatest labor saving devices of today.

YAWN: An honest opinion openly expressed.

WRINKLES: Something other people have. You and I have character lines.

So watcha think? Did we get a smile or two? Good! Now go out and have a terrific day and be thankful for all the good friends you have who will support you through thick or thin. I hope you have a fantastic 2004 and please remember, don't sweat the little things.

Let the Chips Fall Where They May – March 4, 2004

To the editor:

I have some good news for people who like chocolate. I have some very important data on chocolates that you always wanted to know about but didn't know who to ask.

While there are a lot of men out there who enjoy chocolate, recent data I have seen substantiates the fact that women are more susceptible to eating chocolate than men are. I believe the ratio was 60/40. Oh, what the heck, this information is equally important to all of you so let the chocolate chips fall where they may.

- Chocolate has many preservatives. Preservatives make you look younger.
- Chocolate covered raisins, cherries, orange slices and strawberries all count as fruit, so eat as many as

you want.

- If you've got melted chocolate all over your hands, you're eating it too slowly.
- The problem: How to get two pounds of chocolate home from the store in a hot car. The solution: eat it in the parking lot.
- Diet tip: Eat a chocolate bar before each meal. It'll take the edge off your appetite and you'll eat less.
- If you can't eat all your chocolate, it'll keep in the freezer. But if you can't eat all your chocolate, what's wrong with you?
- If calories are an issue, store your chocolate on the top of the fridge. Calories are afraid of heights, and they will jump out of the chocolate to protect themselves.
- Eat equal amounts of dark chocolate and white chocolate for a balanced diet.
- Money talks. Chocolate sings.
- Put "eat chocolate" at the top of your list of things to do today. That way, at least you'll get one thing done.

So to chocolate lovers everywhere, don't sweat the little things, especially small unwrapped pieces of chocolate in your pocket or purse. But, boy, do they make a heck of a mess.

At Fighting Weight – March 20, 2004

To the editor:

I am very happy to announce that I had my surgery on March 1 and everything is progressing just fine. The important thing is the doctor said he got rid of all the disease and it's just a matter of time until everything will be A-OK.

I want to thank the dozens and dozens of you who sent me cards and best wishes and words of comfort and encouragement. I also want to thank those of you who visited me and all who telephoned me your "get wells." I am positive the surgery was successful largely because many, many of you told me personally you would remember me in your prayers. It worked!

They say some good comes from everything. Although I have temporarily (I hope) lost my taste buds and appetite, due to some of the medicines, I have lost a few pounds and am now down to my fighting weight, whatever that means. I really should have gained weight from all the delicious meals my friends and neighbors sent in. One thing for sure, the freezer is full of leftover dinners for future enjoyment. Thanks to all of the gourmet cooks!

I want all of you to know that God has been extremely good to me and has given me an abundance of good friends. Thanks again to each and every one of you and please remember – when my ship comes in, we'll all go for a boat ride. In the meantime, keep a smile on your face, a song in your heart and be good to everyone – especially yourself, because you deserve it.

Kids Have Interesting View of Old, New Testament – April 11, 2004

To the editor:

Recently, as I was eating breakfast, 8 a.m. Midland time and 7:00 a.m. Texas time, one of my Texas granddaughters, Kaitlyn Rose, called and said, "Hi Papa Joe!" I was very surprised because she is not a morning person and doesn't have much to say until about noon time.

She said, "Papa Joe, I love you very much and I have a quote, which I think is from Matthew, that I would like to give to you this morning."

I don't know if I remember it verbatim, but it went something like this, "In the same way you let your light shine before others that they may see your good work, will give glory to your father in heaven." Wow, what a beautiful thing to hear the first thing in the morning, eh?

Needless to say, that quote kind of jarred me awake and reminded me of some of the great things kids have to say from time to time. Always innocent and uninhibited – that's why they are so special.

Recently I read an article about some kids in an elementary school who were asked some questions about the Old and New Testament. The Bible were their answers and have not been retouched or corrected – i.e. incorrect spelling has been left in. Try these on for size:

- Adam and Eve were created from an apple tree. Noah's wife was called Joan of Ark. Noah built an ark, which the animals come onto in pears.
- Lot's wife was a pillar of salt by day, but a ball of fire by night.
- The first commandment was when Eve told Adam to eat the apple.
- Moses died before he reached Canada. Then Joshua led the Hebrews in the battle of Geritol.
- The greatest miracle in the Bible is when Joshua told his son to stand still and he obeyed him.
- Solomon, one of David's sons, had 300 wives and 700 porcupines.
- Jesus was born because Mary had an immaculate contraption.

Only two thoughts come to mind – "Out of the mouths of babes!" and be happy, enjoy life, keep a positive attitude, be good to each other, don't sweat the little things and have a blessed and happy day.

Definitions a Mother Can Love – May 9, 2004

To the editor:

Hurray! Hurray! The ninth of May – that's Mother's Day! On previous Mother's days I have told you about real moms "who don't want to know what the vacuum cleaner just picked up." I have also told you what my mother taught me, "If you fall off that thin and break you neck, don't come running to me." Aren't mothers so very, very wonderful?

Now, what 's the proper name for the wife of my nephew? Niece-in-law? Anyway, this very nice lady, who lives in Washington State, recently sent me a "Glossary for Moms." I thoroughly enjoyed them and, as such, I would like to pass on some of this enjoyment to readers.

- Dumbwaiter: One who asks if the kids would like to order dessert.
- Feedback: The inevitable result when your baby doesn't appreciate the strained carrots.
- Full name: What you call your child when you're mad at him.
- Grandparents: The people who think your children are wonderful even though they're sure you're not raising them right.
- Independent: How we want our children to be as long as they do everything we say.
- Ow: The first word spoken by children with older siblings.
- Puddle: A small body of water that draws small bodies wearing dry shoes into it.
- Show off: A child who is more talented than your own.
- Sterilize: What you do to your first baby's pacifier by boiling it and to your last baby's pacifier by blowing on it.
- Whodunit: None of the kids living in your house.

Now that you're aware of these terms, here's what I would like to suggest you do on Mother's Day. Give your mom a big hug and kiss and tell her how much you love and appreciate her. We all know that sometimes moms an be stern and a little strict, but they soften up when hugged and kissed.

Happy Mother's Day to wonderful mothers and grandmothers everywhere.

Famous Quotes Tickle Funny Bone – May 2, 2004

To the editor:

Last July, I sent a letter to the editor on golf quotes by several famous people. I even included some quotes by non-famous people, such as myself. Here's a couple of examples: "If I hit it right, it's a slice. If I hit it to the left, it's a hook. If I hit it straight, it's a miracle." And, "It's poor sportsmanship to pick up a lost golf ball while they are still rolling."

Anyway, now I have become the fortunate recipient of several non golf quotes made by famous people. Let's see if any of these will tickle your funny bone.

- Santa Claus has the right idea: visit people only once a year – Victor Borge

- I once had a rose named after me and I was very flattered. But I was not pleased to read the description in the catalog. "No good in a bed, but fine up against a wall." – Eleanor Roosevelt
- I was married by a judge. I should have asked for a jury. – Groucho Marx
- Only Irish coffee provides in a single glass all four essential food groups: alcohol, caffeine, sugar and fat. – Alex Levine
- My luck is so bad that if I bought a cemetery, people would stop dying. – Ed Furgol
- Until I was 13, I thought my name was "shut up." – Joe Namath
- I don't feel old. I don't feel anything until noon. Then it's time for my nap. – Bob Hope
- I never drink water because of the disgusting things hat fish do in it – W.C. Fields

O.K. whatcha think? I may not be famous but I still would like to put in my two cents worth. I believe life would be a lot less stressful if we would all lighten up, have a good sense of humor, think positive, be happy, smile and, please, don't sweat the little things.

Today's a Gift – April 2, 2004

To the editor:

I have always been a proponent of "live for today" – yesterday is history, tomorrow is a mystery but today is the present – the present – a gift from God. However, that doesn't mean we can't reminisce and think about the good old days.

An Italian friend of mine recently sent me some "comments of the 50's" that gave me a few flashbacks and several chuckles. I think some of your senior readers will also enjoy them.

I also think the younger generation will now know we were not fibbing when we say it was tough when we were kids. We had to walk five miles to school every day, even in the deep snow and walk was all uphill – going and coming. Only kidding kids – now, everyone, get ready for your history lesson.

- "If cigarettes keep going up in price, I'm going to quit. A quarter a pack is ridiculous."
- "Did you hear the post office is thinking about charging a dime just to mail a letter?"
- "I'll tell you one thing, if things keep going the way they are, it's going to be impossible to buy a week's worth of groceries for $20."
- "If they raise the minimum wage to $1, nobody will be able to hire outside help at the store."
- "When I first started driving, who would have thought gas would someday cost 25 cents a gallon? Guess we'd be better off leaving the car in the garage."
- "I read the other day some scientist thinks it's possible to put a man on the moon by the end of the century. They even have some fellows called astronauts preparing for it down in Texas."
- "I never thought I would see the day all our appliances would be electric … they are even making electric typewriters now."
- "The drive-in restaurant is convenient in nice weather, but I seriously doubt they will ever catch on."
- "There is no sense going to Detroit or Chicago anymore for a weekend. It costs nearly $15 a night to stay in a hotel."
- "No one an afford to be sick any more; $35 a day in the hospital is too rich for my blood."
- "If they think I'll pay 50 cents for a hair cut, forget it.

Now, wasn't that educational – for both generations? Keep a smile on your face, a song in your heart, enjoy life, be kind to each other and – please – don't sweat the little things.

When God Speaks, it Makes Sense for People to Listen – June 6, 2004

To the editor:

As most of you are aware, the "snowbirds" are making their trek back to Midland, now that they have found out we have jumped from winter to summer. No spring! Anyway, if you have any snowbird neighbors coming back from Arizona, ask them to tell you about the "God Speaks" billboards.

The billboards, which are getting a lot of attention along the highways in Arizona, have a plain black background with white text. There is no fine print, nor sponsoring organization included. I would like to give you a few of the comments that an Arizona newspaper recently listed. Enjoy:

- Tell the kids I love them – God
- Let's meet at my house Sunday before the game – God
- C'mon over and bring the kids – God
- What part of thou shalt not … didn't you understand? – God
- We need to talk – God
- Keep using my name in vain, I'll make the rush hour longer – God
- Loved the wedding, invite me to the marriage – God
- That "love thy neighbor thing" … I meant it – God
- I love you and you and you and you and … God
- Will the road you're on get you to my place? – God
- My way is the highway – God
- Big bang theory, you've got to be kidding – God
- You think it's hot here? - God
- Have you read my No. 1 best seller? There will be a test – God
- Do you have any idea where you're going? – God

And here is my favorite: Don't make me come down there – God

I don't think I'll even try to comment on those masterful words of wisdom other than "God is good, God is great, God is the best."

My words of wisdom are pretty much the same, lighten up, smile, be happy, enjoy life and please, don't sweat the little things.

A Little Kiss or Hug Will Do for Dad – June 16, 2004

To the editor:

Well, we just celebrated Mother's Day so it must be time for us to celebrate Father's Day. I think we all find it a little harder to say nice things about dad, but talk about mom, words of praise just seem to flow out. Mom seems to get most of the love whereas we seem to pick on dad most of the time. Yes, he's tough and can take it but that doesn't mean he still doesn't need lots and lots of love.

As BC once asked, "Why must we celebrate Father's Day?" Mother's Day seems quite enough to celebrate on how we got here?" and all that other ego stuff. Could it be a ploy to make us buy not just one card – but two? But face it folks – it took both of them to make me and you.

Yes, Father's Day doesn't quite get the recognition it deserves so this year I'm going to honor a few special fathers who I'm sure you'll recognize:

PAUL REVERE'S FATHER: "I don't care where you think you have to go, young man, midnight is past your curfew."

HUMPTY DUMPTY'S FATHER: "Humpty, If I've told you once, I've told you a hundred times not to sit on that wall, but would you listen to me?"

NAPOLEON'S FATHER: "All right Napoleon. Take your hand out of there and let me see what you're hiding."

MONA LISA'S FATHER – "After all that money your mother and I spent on braces, is that the biggest smile you an give us?"

GEORGE WASHINGTON'S FATHER – "The next time I catch you throwing money across the river, you an kiss your allowance goodbye!"

THOMAS EDISON'S FATHER – Of course I'm proud of your inventions, Thomas. Now turn off that light and get to bed!"

Many years ago, my youngest daughter Sara gave a little speech at my retirement party and I can vividly remember her using the old saying, "Anyone an be a father, but it takes a special person to be called DAD." What a nice warm fuzzy I got. So, too all you "DADS" out there have a very happy and special Father's Day! Not it's up to the rest of us to help him by telling him how much we love and appreciate him and make sure we tell him how thankful we are for him for carrying us on his shoulders most of our lives. A little hug and kiss wouldn't hurt him either. Everyone needs a warm fuzzy from time to time!!

Bad Hair Coming

To the editor:

I think we all have "bad hair" days from time to time, but recently I have had a deluge of them. I'm beginning to wonder what I have done to offend the good hair gods.

If you folks see me out there and I look a little frazzled, don't stare, just say "Hi Papa Joe" and keep going on your way. Only kidding, I always have time to talk to my friends.

Thank goodness though I do adhere to my principal philosophy "not to sweat the little things." However, I have really been tested to the limit a couple of times lately.

My minor trials and tribulations have prompted me to bring a little humor into your lives. I would like to pass on to you a couple of things I have read on how you can tell when you're going to have a bad hair day:

- Your boss tells you not to bother to take your coat off.
- You jump out of bed in the morning and you miss the floor.
- You want to put on the clothes you wore to the party last night and you can't find them.
- The bird singing outside your window is a buzzard.
- Your blind date turns out to be your ex-husband.
- You walk to work and find your dress is stuck in the back of your dress.
- Your income tax return check bounces.
- You all your answering service and they tell you it's none of your business.
- You wake up to discover your waterbed has broken and then you discover you don't have a waterbed.
- Your bar of Ivory soap sinks …

So, I say unto you, keep a smile on your face – things could be worse, although it doesn't seem like it at the time. Get the stress out of your life, lighten up, keep a good sense of humor and "don't sweat the little things."

Old "Cheers" Story Recalled – June 21, 2004

To the editor:

Now I know why I'm getting old so fast – I can't keep up with everything that's going on in my life. Recently I became the recipient of a humorous beer story. (Why can't I ever be the recipient of a lottery winner?)

Anyway, I thought, boy, this would make a good letter to the editor; but then I remembered I had "recently" sent in a letter on beer as requested by the boys at the Big B. Just for the heck of it I decided to check the date of that "recent" letter, and would you believe I sent it in nearly two years ago. Tempus Fugit!

My original letter on beer was some quotes by famous people such as Benjamin Franklin. ("Beer is proof that God loves us and wants us to be happy.") Then Frank Sinatra said "I feel sorry for people who don't drink. When they wake up in the morning, that's as good as they're going to feel all day."

Now, my story! How many of you remember the TV show "Cheers"? Always one of my favorite shows and my two favorite characters were Cliff and Norm. One day at Cheers Cliff was explaining the buffalo theory to his buddy Norm. Here's how it went: "Well, ya see, Norm, it's like this … A herd of buffaloes can only move as fast as the slowest buffalo. And when the herd is hunted, it is the slowest and weakest ones at the back that are killed first. This natural selection is good for the herd as a whole, because the general speed and health of the whole group keeps improving by the regular killing of the weakest members. In much the same way, the human brain can only operate as fast as the slowest brain cells. Excessive intake of alcohol, as we know, kills brain cells. But naturally, it attacks the slowest and weakest brain cells first. In this way, regular consumption of beer eliminates the weaker brain cells, making the brain a faster and more efficient machine. That's why you always feel smarter after a few beers.

Remember folks, this was a TV show and although a humorous story, it is not to be taken seriously. This is not an endorsement for beer drinking and should be taken with a grain of salt. Like I said last two years ago, if you're going to put this salt in your beer, make sure it's non-alcoholic beer!

Like I've said many times, "Don't sweat the little things," but if you get thirsty, have a tall glass of iced tea.

Do You Remember When? – July 8, 2004

To the editor:

I am always preaching "live for today" and that is the practical thing to do, but sometimes my mind wonders off and I start thinking about the good old days. Just thinking about some of the things that happened years ago brings a big smile to my face and makes me feel good all over – a nice, warm fuzzy feeling. Know what I mean?

I normally write my letters to include all ages, but today I think I'll digress and slant my message more toward the elderly crowd (the younger group and read this and maybe they'll have a better appreciation of what us old folks had to go through to survive).

The question I have today is "Do you remember when …"?

- A quarter was a decent allowance?
- You'd reach into a muddy gutter for a penny?
- Decisions were made by going "eeny-meeny-miney-moe?"
- Catching fireflies could happily occupy an entire evening?
- It wasn't odd to have two or three "best friends?"
- The worst thing you could catch from the opposite sex was "cooties?"
- Having a weapon in school mean being caught with a slingshot?
- A foot of snow was a dream come true?
- "Oly-oly-oxen-free" made perfect sense?
- Baseball cards in the spokes transformed any bike into a motorcycle?
- Taking drugs meant orange-flavored chewable aspirin?
- Water balloons were the ultimate weapon?

If you remember most or all of the above, then you have lived! We did have a lot of fun and good times in those days. Don't you just wish, just once, you could slip back in time and savor the slower pace, and share it with the children of today?

Not to worry, though, because we know that life goes on and we just keep flowing along with it. Most importantly, we don't sweat the little things in life. Do we?

The Truth About Aging – August 23, 2004

To the editor:

There are many quotes on "how you can tell you're getting old." I have avoided sending them in a letter to the editor, not that they aren't all true but because they are mostly old clichés. Instead I would like to send you a few of the more philosophical quotes for your consideration. Especially those of you who are considering or contemplating joining the geriatric stage of life.

- Eventually you will reach a point when you stop lying about your age and start bragging about it.
- The older we get, the fewer things seem worth waiting for.
- Some people try to turn back their odometers. Not me, I want people to know "why" I look this way. I've traveled a long way and some of the roads weren't paved.
- When you are dissatisfied and would like to go back to your youth, think of algebra.
- You know you're getting old when everything either dried up or leaks.
- You start to wondering how you got over the hill without reaching the top.
- One of the things no one tells you about aging is that it is such a nice change from being young.
- One must wait until evening to see how splendid the day has been.
- Being young is beautiful but being old is comfortable.

- Long ago, when men cursed and beat the ground with sticks, it was called witchcraft. Today it's called golf.

And, finally, if you don't learn to laugh at trouble, you won't have anything to laugh at when you are old.

Well, what more can I say, as a senior, other than "it's the truth, the whole truth and nothing but the truth." Since there isn't anything I can do about it, I shall continue to enjoy every day that comes along and not sweat any of those little things. I would suggest that all of you, regardless of your age, do the same thing, with a smile on your face and a positive attitude. God bless!

True Beauty Comes From Within – July 31, 2004

To the editor:

First of all, I would like to thank Channing Johnson, the photographer who took the picture of my beautiful wife and I, and the Midland Daily News for printing it. The only thing I would add to the article is that I have been married to my wife for close to 55 years and I love her more with each passing day.

To be sure, the picture of old Papa Joe wasn't too flattering, but as I always say, "Don't sweat the little things." Besides, true beauty comes from within.

Quite often people will ask me why I visit my wife so frequently when she doesn't know if I'm there or not. First of all, we don't really know if she knows I'm there or not. Regardless, I know I'm there! Maybe I do it selfishly because it gives me an enormous amount of satisfaction, fulfillment and happiness to visit and touch her. Besides, who knows, maybe one of these visits she might just give me one of her beautiful smiles and I wouldn't want to miss that, would I?

I especially want to thank the MDN for publishing the picture because it gives me another opportunity to express my feelings on "where's the family?" As most of you may remember, I'm referring to a letter to the editor dated Nov. 29, 2003, referring to visitations – or lack of – by people to their loved ones, relatives or friends in nursing homes.

So, what's your excuse this summer, folks? Is it too hot to drive 10-20 minutes to visit them? You can't be on vacation all summer. Too much housework or yardwork to do? You can always take a 15- to 20-minute break and visit them. Regardless, I bet you come up with some kind of excuse not to visit them. Regardless, I bet you come up with some kind of excuse not to visit them. Shame on you! Doesn't your conscience bother you at night when you go to bed?

I'm not trying to be cruel or insulting. I just want to shake people up a little to the point where they may listen to my pleas and make that visit to the nursing home. I'm sure they will find it a win-win situation.

So please folks, come on and make my day. Make plans, today, to go visit them – positively – one day next week. I'll be looking for you.

Have a great day and nice visit!

Morning is a Train Wreck – August 5, 2004

To the editor:

Recently in a letter to the editor I mentioned I had a bad hair day. Many people wanted to know what had frazzled ole Papa Joe so much since I don't normally sweat the little things. Let me clarify the matter:

It started when my breakfast oatmeal, raisins, walnuts and milk curdled while I was heating it.

I decided to go to the store for fresh milk. Stopped in neighbor's driveway first to check on the sprinklers sine I am housesitting while they're on vacation. I got too close to their second car in the driveway and broke the rear view mirror on the Volvo. Cost $55.12.

Finally had breakfast and decided to trim tree in front of the dining room window. Did an excellent job – except for one small branch sticking up. Got on the ladder to cut off, but got the electric clippers too close to the cord and cut it in half.

Radio in garage went off so I knew I had blown a fuse. Went down to the basement to reset the fuse box and found a large puddle of clear liquid at the bottom of the stairs. Panic set in because the way things were going I thought for sure I had a ruptured water line. Luckily [?] only a can of sprite in a 12-pack exploded – I think.

After cleaning up that sticky mess, I decided it was time to wash all the outside windows. Not taking any chances, I went into the house to make sure ALL the windows were closed – tightly!

I placed my ladder and extended the water hose to the side of the house I was going to start on. I put the large container of Windex Outdoors Cleaner on the end of the water hose and placed it on top of the ladder. Went to the water faucet, turned it on, went back to the ladder and climbed to the top. I picked up the hose with the container of Windex and lifted it to spray the first upstairs window. Guess what? Yep, the container of Windex fell off and to the ground. Then I asked myself, am I having fun yet?

Agitated – don't sweat the little things! – I slowly climbed down the ladder, not wishing to fall and break my neck. By the time I got down on the ground, the container was more than half empty – or if that half full? Regardless, whoopee!

Now what? Decided to go to the store and replenish my window cleaner. As I backed out of the driveway, one of my neighbors who was aware of my problems asked me where I was going. When I told him, he suggested I go to the Boulevard instead.

Excellent idea, things were starting to look better. So instead of turning right I turned left and found myself having a nice juicy hamburger and a tall cool glass of iced tea.

YES, all of the above happened before noon time! Then I went home and had a nice quiet and peaceful nap.

Unfortunately, I started off the next day having another "bad hair" day, but I'll tell you about that another time. In the meantime, don't sweat the little things. Believe me, they can and do get bigger and worse sometimes!

If Only Politicians had Will's Wisdom – August 27, 2004

To the editor:

Reading all those political letters to the editor recently got me thinking about William Penn Adair Rogers or plain old Will Rogers to us old timers. Will lived from 1879-1935, was an actor and probably the greatest political sage and humorist this country has ever known.

Since a lot of people may not know much about Will, I decided to pass on a few of his political quotes for their edification and enjoyment. Here goes:

- "I don't belong to an organized party – I am a Democrat."
- "I don't make jokes, I just watch the government and report the facts."
- "There's no trick to being a humorist when you have half the government working for you."
- "Income tax has made more liars out of the American people than golf has."
- "The man with the best job in the country is the vice president. All he has to do is get up every morning and say, 'How's the President?'"

How's that for a starter? Now how about a few of his sage comments, that are down to earth just like Will was. I'm not sure but I may have used a few of these quotes in the past. Regardless, I'm sure you will enjoy reading them again.

- "Never slap a man who's chewing tobacco."
- "There are two theories to arguing with a woman – neither works."
- "If you find yourself in a hole, quit digging."
- "Never kick a cow chip on a hot day."
- "Always drink upstream from the herd."
- "Letting the cat outta the bag is a whole lot easier than puttin' it back."
- "After eating an entire bull, a mountain lion felt so good he started roaring. He kept it up until a hunter came along and shot him. The moral: When you're full of bull, keep your mouth shut!"

Well, what did you think? Don't you wish some of our modern politicians had the wisdom and common sense of some of our old timers? Oh well, like they say, some days you're the pigeon and some days you're the statue. But, don't worry about it – enjoy life, smile, be happy, think positive, take it one day at a time and don't sweat the little things.

Grandparents are Something to Celebrate – September 24, 2004

To the editor:

Did all of you know that we celebrate Grandparents Day on September 24? Well, we do, so start celebrating and giving out all those hugs you have been hoarding. Everyone is welcome to join in the fun.

Did you ever wonder what it was about grandparents that captivates a child's love and admiration? Let's see if we can find out!

A niece of mine in Florida, and a grandmother herself recently sent me an article describing what a grandparent was. The comments in the article were taken from notes by a class of 8-year-olds. I think you will agree that their comments capture much of the grandparenting magnetism. So let's see what the kids had to say about grandparents.

- Grandparents are a lady and a man who have no children of their own. They like other people's children.
- A grandfather is a man's grandmother.
- When they take us for walks, they slow down past things like pretty leaves and caterpillars.
- They show us and talk to us about the color of the flowers and also why we should not step on cracks.
- They don't say, "Hurry up."
- They wear glasses and funny underwear.
- They can take their teeth and gums out.
- When they read to us, they don't skip. They don't mind if we ask for the same story over again.
- They know we should have snack time before bedtime and they say prayers with us every time, and kiss us even when we've acted bad.

Finally, a 6-year-old was asked where his grandparents lived. "Oh, they live at the airport, and when we want them, we just go get them. Then when we're dong having them visit us, we take them back to the airport."

Did those comments bring a smile to your face? I'll bet they did and I'll also bet you had a few grandparent thoughts of your own. My thoughts are of those nice big hugs and kisses and that nice warm fuzzy feeling I used to get. Enough said?

I would like to tell one quick grandma story before I close. The teacher told her first grade class to put their hands over their hearts. Lil' Joe put his hand on his fanny. The teacher said, "That's not your heart Joe." "Yes, it is, teacher, because every time my grandma picks me up, she taps me there and says, 'Bless your little heart Joe.'"

God bless each and every grandparent and may you keep healthy and happy!

Too Much Stuff – October 12, 2004

To the editor:

Friends, I think I have finally gotten to the point lately where I don't know what I have. Does that make sense to you? I'm finding things I didn't know I had or where they came from. I don't know if it has anything to do with "seniority" or maybe I'm just accumulating too much "stuff." (How do you like that new word – "seniority?")

Case in point. Recently, as I was leafing through some of my "stuff," I found a list of quotes I had jotted down, but I have no idea when I wrote them or where I got them. Anyway, I think they are kind of humorous, so why not make good use of them and share them with readers. Enjoy.

- If a man's home is his castle, he should learn to clean it.
- Few women admit their age. Few men act it.
- If you can't change your mind, are you sure you have one?
- As long as there are tests, there will always be prayers in public schools.
- If there is a tourist season, how come we can't shoot them?
- I will defend, to your death, my right to my opinion.

- Mothers of teens know why some animals eat their young.
- Everyone seems normal until you get to know them.
- If you wake up breathing – congratulations – you have another chance.
- My sex life isn't dead, but the buzzards are circling.
- How do you prevent sagging? Just eat until the wrinkles fill out.
- I've still got it, but unfortunately no one wants it.

Well, whatcha think? Quite a potpourri of words of wisdom, eh? I know all of you connoisseurs of the finer things in life enjoyed them as you always do.

As I sit here thoroughly enjoying these tidbits myself, I often wonder why so many people take life so seriously, when we have such a short time on this earth.

I guess it's "each to his own," but come on folks, why not grab that merry-go-round of life as the world goes around. Be happy, enjoy life, smile, live for today with a positive attitude and give someone a hug today. And, oh, yes, don't sweat the little stuff!

Cobwebs are No Problem – October 20, 2004

To the editor:

Being a caregiver for many years, due to my wife's illness, I have learned to be the chief cook and bottle washer in my home. Those two terms sound quite innocuous, but they encompass many, many duties and responsibilities that have to be done day-in and day-out.

Since my responsibilities got to be so overwhelming, I have had to evaluate my position and prioritize my house duties. I thought your readers might like to know what I have done to alleviate my work load.

- I don't wash windows because I love birds and don't want one to fly into a clean window and get hurt. (I am compassionate.)
- I don't wax floors because I'm terrified guests will slip and hurt themselves and I would feel terrible – and they might sue me. (I am careful and poor.)
- I don't mind the dust bunnies because they are good company. I have named most of them and they agree with everything I say. (I am imaginative.)
- I don't disturb cobwebs because I want every creature to have a home of its own. Besides, I enjoy watching spiders. (I am kind.)
- I don't spring clean because I love all the seasons and don't want the others to get jealous. (I am fair-minded.)
- I don't plant a garden because I don't want to get in God's way. He is an excellent designer. (I am courteous.)
- I don't put things away because my family will never find them when they come to visit. (I am considerate.)
- I don't do gourmet meals when friends come over because I don't want to stress out over what they serve me when (and if!) they invite me over to dinner.
- I don't iron because I believe them when they say "permanent press." (I am trusting.)
- I don't stress out much on anything (don't sweat the little things) because "A Type" personalities die young and Ii want to stick around and become a wrinkled up crusty old man.

So, unless I win the lottery or can get someone to help me with the household chores, I guess that's the way it has to be. I will continue though, to the best of my ability, to live one day at a time, with a positive attitude, a smile on my face and promise not to sweat the little things.

Some More Wisdom – October 31, 2004

To the editor:

I was going to send your readers a list of ponderings that I have been saving, but guess what? A shirt-tail relative of mine living down in Arkansas sent me some words of wisdom that I haven't seen before.

So, guess what my first thought was? Send them on to the MDN readers who enjoy getting a little knowledge once in a while. So, get out your cap and gown kids, here's some more wisdom I'm passing on for your enlightenment.

- Never read the fine print. There ain't no way you're going to like it.
- If you let a smile be your umbrella, then most likely your butt will get soaking wet.
- People who live in glass houses should make love in the basement.
- To err is human. To forgive – highly unlikely.
- The trouble with bucket seats is that not everyone has the same size bucket.
- Money cannot buy happiness – but somehow it's more comfortable to cry in a Porsche than a Hyundai.
- The only two things we do with greater frequency as we get older are urinate and attend funerals.
- Drinking makes some husbands see double and feel single.
- Living in a nudist colony takes all the fun out of Halloween.
- Do you realize that in about 40 years, we'll have thousands of old ladies running around with tattoos?

There, now don't you feel a whole lot smarter than you did before? Now I want all of you to start boning up on your reading because the next time I'm going to give you a quiz on some really tough questions I have that I haven't been able to find the answers to. In the meantime I'm not going to sweat the little things because I know you'll give me the answers I'm looking for. In the meantime, give someone a hug!!!

Musings – November 15, 2004

To the editor:

One of my favorite pastimes, when I have the time, is to go through my old ponderings or conundrums or whatever else you want to call them. I get a lot of enjoyment and laughter in reading them. Occasionally I start feeling guilty because I'm not sharing them with readers. I don't want to hurt your feelings and I do want to share my happiness with you. So, dear friends, here are some really good questions I would like you to ponder. Please, just don't strain your brain.

- Does a clean house indicate there is a broken computer in it?
- Is there ever a day when mattresses are not on sale?
- Why do people constantly return to the refrigerator with hopes that something new to eat will have materialized?
- How do dead bugs get into closed light fixtures?
- Why is it that every time you try to catch something that's falling off the table you always manage to knock something else over?
- Is it true that the only difference between a yard sale and trash pickup is how close to the road the stuff is placed?
- In the winter, why do we keep the house as warm as it was in the summer when we complained about the heat?
- How come you never hear father-in-law jokes?
- If at first you don't succeed, shouldn't you try doing it like your wife told you to?
- The statistics on sanity are that one in four of every American is suffering from some sort of mental illness. Think of your best friends, if they're okay, then it's you!
- If carrots are good for the eyes, how come I see so many dead rabbits on the highway?
- Why is it that most nudists are people you don't want to see naked?

Well, what did you think? I hope my little peace offering brought a few smiles to your face. I am always willing to share with my friends! That also goes for my hugs – so if you see me out and about and would like a hug, just open your arms and I'll know you want one. Until then, give someone else a hug.

Remember, keep a smile on your face, a song in your heart and be good to everyone, especially yourself, because you deserve it. And don't sweat the little things, like those leaves in the yard. I don't care what they say, leaves on the ground are not beautiful!

We Should be Thankful Every Day – November 25, 2004

To the editor:

Thanksgiving Day – the only day of the year most people try to give thanks for all the wonderful things that God has bestowed upon us. As I have stated in the past, why celebrate "thanks-giving" only one day of the year? We should be offering up our thanks every day.

Even though we all have so many things to be thankful for, some of us still find time to criticize or complain about things. Why do we feel sorry for ourselves when things could be a whole lot worse for us? If we would just take a minute to look around, we would all find out how fortunate we are.

So you notice a few gray hairs in the mirror and a slightly receding hairline – think of the cancer patient going through chemotherapy who has no hair to examine in the mirror!

See what I mean? And we all could list many more examples, but why dwell on the negative things? A positive attitude will help us realize how fortunate we are and the many things we have to be thankful for.

How about this beautiful country we live in? The warm bed we sleep in on a cold night? A soft touch or hug from our children or grandchildren? The warm food we eat every day? The love of our family and friends?

They say some good comes from everything regardless how bad it is or was. My wife's illness is an example – it has taught me to be patient, tolerant, compassionate, considerate, understanding and many other good qualities of life. Every time I visit my wife and her fellow residents at the nursing home, I realize just how many things I have to be thankful for. Margie and her friends have made me a much better person.

I am especially thankful that God has given me 80 years of a good, healthy happy life, with a positive attitude, a good sense of humor (I think!), and the ability to not sweat the little things, while I try to keep a smile on my face – most of the time.

So dear friends, I wish the same good fortune for all of you and your families. I also want to thank you for the friendship you have shared with me over the years. I wish you good health, peace and happiness and hope you have a wonderful Thanksgiving Day with your loving family.

Rules to Live By – December 17, 2004

To the editor:

Recently I was thinking of a couple of topics I wanted to write about when I was reminded of a recent trip to visit my grandson Jakie Joe. Ah ha! One of my favorite topics – young kids and all those wonderful uninhibited remarks and answers they give to adult questions!

So for readers' enjoyment, here are some questions that were put forth on the topic of dating and marriage and their uninhibited and unbiased answers.

WHEN IS IT OK TO KISS SOMEONE?
- "The law says you have to be 18, so I wouldn't want to mess with that." – Curt, age 7
- "The rule goes like this: If you kiss someone, then you should marry them and have kids with them. It's the right thing to do." – Howard, age 8
- "When they're rich." – Pam, age 7

IS IT BETTER TO BE SINGLE OR MARRIED?
- "I don't know which is better, but I'll tell you one thing. I'm never going to have sex with my wife. I don't want to be all grossed out." = Theodore, age 8
- "It's better for girls to be single but not for boys. Boys need someone to clean up after them." – Anita, age 9 (bless you child)

HOW WOULD THE WORLD BE DIFFERENT IF PEOPLE DIDN'T GET MARRIED?
- "There sure would be a lot of kids to explain, wouldn't there?" – Kevin, age 9

HOW WOULD YOU MAKE A MARRIAGE WORK?
- "Tell your wife that she looks pretty, even though she looks like a truck." – Ricky, age 10

WHAT IS THE RIGHT AGE TO GET MARRIED?

- "Twenty-three is the best age because you know the person FOREVER by then." – Camille, age 10
- "No age is good to get married at. You got to be a fool to get married." – Freddie, age 6

HOW CAN A STRANGER TELL IF TWO PEOPLE ARE MARRIED?

- "You might have to guess based on whether they seem to be yelling at the same kids." – Derrick, age 8

WHAT DO YOU THINK YOUR MOM AND DAD HAVE IN COMMON?

- "Both don't want any more kids." – Lori, age 8

This letter is for my buddy Jakie Joe. As I write it I'm thinking that the next time I do something like this I am going to ask Jakie for his opinion on the topics. It should be interesting to see what he has to say.

Let's Make Midland the Friendliest City in Michigan – January 6, 2005

To the editor:

I live such a good clean life that I don't normally make any New Year's resolutions. However, this year I have decided to make one resolution and I am going to let readers in on it as I'm going to need their help to make it happen. So, what is my New Year's resolution? To make Midland the friendliest city in Michigan! Yep, and I firmly believe "we" can do it.

I believe one of the biggest problems in the country today is that most people are wrapped up in themselves and live in their own little worlds, afraid to expose themselves to the rest of us. Look around the next time you're out shopping and observe your fellow human beings. People hardly ever speak to each other, or smile or even nod their heads.

Really, when was the last time you passed someone and they smiled or said hello? You would probably remember if it happened because it would have made you feel good, right? But why do we have to wait for someone to say "Hi" or give us a smile? Let's be the givers and get double the pleasure by giving smiles and saying "Hi, how are you?" Remember, 'tis better to give than receive.

So here's my plan, which I would like to call, "Hi H.A.Y." or "Hi, How Are You?" I'm sure those four words and a big smile will accomplish great and wonderful results.

So, how do we accomplish this goal? Starting today and every day from now on, every time you pass someone, regardless of where you are, say, with a nice smile on your face, "Hi, how are you?" I'll bet, if we diligently continue with this plan, it won't be too long before someone beats us to giving of this greeting. Then both people can start laughing and be happy the plan is working.

It's essential that you also get your family and friends involved to help us. You will have to explain what our plans are before they begin but I'll bet if you give them a big hug, it won't be hard to convince them to help us. Give it a try, what have you got to lose?

Whatever you do, you can't be shy, timid or bashful. Put that smile on your face and speak up, "Hi, how are you?" I think you are really going to be surprised at how good it's going to make you feel. I know because I have been doing a little practicing.

So, are you wonderful people going to be part of my New Year's resolution? I certainly hope so. I have never been afraid of failure before because that word is not in my vocabulary, but I definitely am going to need a lot of help with this one.

So, let's all get out there with those nice big smiles and your "Hi, how are yous" and "make Midland the friendliest city in Michigan."

P.S. Everyone, be prepared out there, we're coming after you! You had better put a smile on your face, a song in your heart and start being good to everyone, especially yourself, because you deserve it. Smile everyone!

Just Say Hi – January 25, 2005

To the editor:

Hi, how are you? It's been a couple of weeks since our plan was launched to make "Midland the Friendliest City in Michigan." How are you doing? I'm doing great and having a good time. I hope you're enjoying yourself because I'm having a blast.

One thing is for sure, when I walk into one of my favorite haunts now, you'll know I'm there because everyone yells out "Hi Papa Joe, how are you?" Lots of big smiles, laughs and good humor – just what we're looking for. Keep it up!

I would like to ask all of you not to get discouraged or disappointed. Rome was not built in a day nor is our plan going to happen overnight. We have to be patient and keep plugging away, one day at a time. It will happen. "We" can do it!

Now, let's all get back out there with our best smile and "Hi, how are yous" and let the people around town know what we're doing, "Making Midland the Friendliest City in Michigan."

Think positive with a smile on your face and please remember the more "Hi, how are yous" you give out, the more "highs" you are going to get in your life.

The Value of Time – February 8, 2005

To the editor:

In the past I have referred to some of my grandkids but I don't believe I have ever mentioned Gretchen Marie. Gretchen is my 14-year-old granddaughter who lives in Texas. Gretchen used to be involved in competitive cheerleading but gave it up to be able to be an honor student. Cheerleading is very big in Texas. I don't know if she ever made the state championship but if not, she came very close.

Anyway, just the other day Gretchen sent me some very profound quotes on values of time and the many things that can happen in any time frame of our lives. I don't know where Gretchen got them but I do know they are more than worthwhile to pass on to readers. Enjoy.

- To realize the value of 10 years, ask a newly divorced couple.
- To realize the value of four years, ask a graduate.
- To realize the value of one year, ask a student who has failed an exam.
- To realize the value of nine months, ask a mother who has given birth to a premature baby.
- To realize the value of one week, ask an editor of a weekly newspaper.
- To realize the value of one hour, ask the lovers who are waiting to meet.
- To realize the value of one minute, ask a person who has missed a train, bus or plane.
- To realize the value of one second, ask a person who has survived an accident.
- To realize the value of one millisecond, ask a person who has won a silver medal in the Olympics.
- To realize the value of a sister, ask someone who doesn't have one.
- To realize the value of a friend, lose one.

The way Papa Joe sees it, time waits for no one, so treasure every moment you have. You will treasure it even more if you share it with someone special. Take it one day at a time with a good, positive attitude and don't sweat the little things. Just remember, life is like riding a bicycle – you don't fall off unless you stop peddling!

You Don't Have to Sweat to be Efficient – January 12, 2005

To the editor:

I recently gave a talk to a very nice, large group of people and besides the humor I tried to instill in my speech, I also tried to incorporate some words of wisdom I have learned in being the man of the household.

This responsibility is not of my own choosing, but because my wife had to retire to a nursing home.

So, not only am I the man of the house, Ii am also the chief cook and bottle washer. They say a woman's work is never done – well believe me, a woman and a man's work combined is never, never, ever done!!!!

Since I have had to assume both roles, I am constantly looking for ways on how to be more efficient and save time with my domestic duties. I am making some progress and as such, in the interest of your readers, I thought I would pass on a few of my innovations.

I used to wash and change my bed sheets and pillow cases every week, but then one day I asked myself,

"Why wash the bedding every week when I only use one side of the bed?" Using logic, and my brilliancy, I decided to sleep on one side of the bed for a week and then sleep on the other side the following week. Pretty clever eh? Now I only have to wash the bedding every two weeks. Look at all the soap and water I'm saving!!

Oh, if I do feel like I have to sleep on the same side of the bed all the time – no problem – after the first week I just rotate the sheets and pillow cases!

Another time saver I have started using is with the bath towel laundering. I used to put my bath towels in the dirty laundry every other day. Then one day I asked myself, why? (As you may have gathered I talk to myself quite frequently – that's how I get most of my information!)

When I take a nice warm shower, using lots of soap and warm water, I have a nice clean body. Right? Right! Why then should I wash the towel more frequently than after every four baths?!

I guess I could shower only every other day and then I wouldn't have to launder my towels so frequently. The only problem with this idea is, I think my friends would start calling me Stinky Joe instead of Papa Joe.

One thing for sure, I'm definitely not going to "sweat" the little things, like how often I'm going to wash my bath towels, because if I did I would probably work up a sweat and have to take more showers!!!

Peace and good will to all of you, my good friends.

How Good We Have It – February 22, 2005

To the editor:

Many years ago when I was thinking about retiring, some of my friends asked me what I was going to do when I really did retire. Without hesitation, my response was, "I'm going to get out of Midland in the winter time and go somewhere it's nice and warm." That's exactly what my sweet Marjorie and I did for many years until she got too sick to travel.

Recently, my son John, who has lived in Florida for many years, surprised me and came home for my 80th birthday celebration. One evening several of us were talking about how nice it is in Florida in the wintertime but oh, so very hot and miserable in the summertime.

One of the ladies who had never been to Florida asked John just how hot it gets in the summertime. Since a lot of readers might never have been in Florida in the summertime either, I thought they might be interested in some of John's comments: "It is so hot in Florida in the summertime that …"

- The birds have to use potholders to pull worms out of the ground.
- The trees are whistling for the dogs.
- The best parking place is determined by shade instead of distance.
- Hot water comes out of both taps.
- You can make sun tea instantly.
- The temperature drops below 95 and you feel a little chilly.
- You realize that asphalt has a liquid state.
- The potatoes cook underground, so all you have to do is pull one out, butter, salt and pepper it and start eating.
- The cows are giving evaporated milk.
- Farmers are feeding their chickens crushed ice to keep them from laying boiled eggs.

Now, aren't you glad you know all those things about Florida? If you want my advice, I would suggest you pack a bag immediately and head for Florida before the hot season gets there.

I'm heading to Florida myself. I have volunteered to help the state of Florida and their security program. My job will be to sit on the beach of sunny Naples and be on the lookout for foreign submarines that might attack America.

I did the same thing for several years in the past. I guess I was fortunate not to see any, but I did get a bad sunburn. This year I'm not going to sweat the little things, like a sunburn, because I'm going to take a lot of sunscreen.

The "Whys" of Life – March 17, 2005

To the editor:

I don't know why, but it seems the more mature I become (that's the same as saying "the older I get"), the more "whys" I see in my life. You too? Let me give you a few examples and see if they're on your list. Oh, please note that I am trying to give some "maybes" to answer some of those whys.

- Why are there three tennis balls in a can? You can only play with one and serve with two. Wouldn't it make sense to only have two in a can? (Maybe it's the same as buying a six-pack of beer – you don't have to drink it all at once.)
- Why, on rare occasions when I set the alarm clock, I wake up before the alarm goes off! How does your brain know? (Maybe your brain's telling you it's time to get up and go to the bathroom."
- Why do golfers talk about their bad shots, never about their good ones? (Maybe, like me, they don't make very many good shots to talk about.)
- Another thing, why is it those little pencils on the golf courses, to keep score, don't have erasers? (Boy, if I ever needed an eraser, it was on the golf course.)
- And, Punxsutawney Phil, how does he know when it's Feb. 2 and time to make his appearance? (I keep wondering when Phil first started looking for his shadow and when he made his first appearance. I made my first appearance at Dow Corning on Feb. 2, 1948 – and I'm still looking for my shadow.)
- How about the swallows at San Capistrano? They always leave to migrate on St. John's Day, Oct. 23, and always come back on the same day – St. Joseph's Day, March 19. Why? (Maybe that's the day they put out the bird feed.)

Mentioning St. Joseph's Day always reminds me of St. Patrick's Day which is two days earlier, March 17. I will celebrate St. Patrick's Day the same as usual with my boiled dinner – corned beef, cabbage, carrots, onions, red potatoes and maybe a glass of green beer.

I'll also celebrate St. Joseph's Day with a few prayers to my patron saint and thank God that I am fortunate enough that I have the freedom to make my own decisions and celebrate whatever I want to.

So, I wish each and every one of you a happy St. Patrick and St. Joseph days. Why not celebrate them both and have twice the enjoyment? Now that we've made that decision, we really don't have to sweat the little things, do we?

Letters Inspiring – March 19, 2005

To the editor:

I was recently very surprised when I read the MDN and learned that my good neighbors, Sue and Dick Heiny, had sent in a letter to the editor telling your readers I had had surgery and was home recuperating. They also suggested your readers send me a card of note wishing me a speedy recovery.

They also told my two daughters (my caregivers!) not to tell Papa Joe because it was to be a surprise when the mailman came. Now I know why they didn't give me a copy of the MDN that day.

On my first day home my daughter went out to get the mail and returned with a "few get well cards, Dad." Well that few turned out to be 40 cards and letters. WOW! What a great surprise.

If that weren't a big enough surprise, the next day the mailman brought me another 40 cards, 20 the next day, 20 the next day and as I'm writing this letter, he brought me another 10 cards. 130 cards and letters! Isn't that fantastic?

I'm pretty sure there are more on the way now that people have found out I have been in the hospital and not sitting on the sunny beach in Naples, Florida on the lookout for foreign submarines that might attack America. At least I didn't get a sunburn.

The comments most expressed in the cards and letters, besides "good health and get well soon," were comments on my letters to the editor. Some of you said you were motivated or inspired by my letters, but all of you said you wanted me to keep them coming. I promise to "keep 'em coming" but you'll have to ask the editor to "keep publishing 'em."

Needless to say, I am overwhelmed and flabbergasted by the outpouring of love and kindness given to me. You are all truly wonderful. I have been trying to figure out how I can adequately express my sincere thanks and appreciation to all of you. (Can you believe ole Papa Joe is at a loss for words?)

I'll just say "thanks a million" and I promise you'll all be in my daily thoughts and prayers. God bless you. Please promise me if you see me out and about, let me know and you'll be welcome to one of Papa Joe's big hugs.

Yes, I am taking my medicines and following the doctor's orders and making great progress with my recuperation. And, I promise "not to sweat the little things."

Memories of Burma Shave – April 10, 2005

To the editor:

I have inherited some memorabilia that brought back some fond memories. I think it will also arouse some memories for some of your more mature readers. I would suggest that you younger folks ask your grandma and grandpa to tell you their experiences with the Burma Shave signs.

For those who never saw the Burma Shave signs, here is a quick lesson in our history of the 1930s and 1940s. Before the Interstate highways, when everyone drove on two lane roads, Burma Shave signs would be posted all over the countryside in farmer's fields. They were small red signs with white letters. Five signs, about 100 feet apart, each containing one line of a two line couplet, and the obligatory fifth sign advertising Burma Shave, a popular shaving cream. Here are a few of the actual signs:

- Don't lose your head ... to gain a minute ... you need your head ... your brains are in it. Burma Shave
- Drove too long ... driver snoozing ... what happened next ... is not amusing. Burma Shave
- The midnight ride ... of Paul for beer ... led to a warmer ... hemisphere. Burma Shave
- Around the curve ... lickety-split ... it's a beautiful car ... wasn't it? Burma Shave
- At intersections ... look each way ... a harp sounds nice ... but it's hard to play. Burma Shave
- The one who drives when ... he's been drinking ... depends on you ... to do his thinking. Burma Shave
- Car in ditch ... driver in tree ... the moon was full ... and so was he. Burma Shave

And my all-time favorite:

- Passing school zone ... take it slow ... let our little ... shavers grow. Burma Shave

Do these slogans bring back some memories? If they do, you're older than dirt! But, dirt never did kill anyone, now did it? And, probably one of the reasons some of us have lived this long is that we didn't have to sweat the little things back then!

Some Ramblings to Consider – May 15, 2005

To the editor:

Being an octogenarian – golly, I like the sound of that word. I wonder what I'm going to call myself when I reach 90? Novogenarian? I really don't like the sound of that but since I have 10 years to think about it, I'm not going to worry until then.

Anyway, it seems like lately I'm remembering things that happened years ago. I don't remember where or when I read or heard this quote but it was a long time ago. "As you ramble on through life, whatever be your goal, keep your eye upon the donut and not the hole."

Now, isn't that profound and worth remembering all those years? Or, a waste of brain space? Anyway, I have some great "ramblings" that I would like to pass on to readers for their edification. Try these on for size:

- I was recently thinking about how a status symbol of today is those cell phones that everyone has clipped on. I can't afford one, so I'm wearing my garage door opener.
- I spent a fortune on deodorants before I finally realized that people didn't like me anyway.
- I often think about old age and have decided that I still have something on the ball – I'm just too tired to bounce it!

- I also once thought about making a fitness movie for folks my age – I was going to call it "Pumping Rust."
- Have you ever noticed that when people see a cat's litter box, they always say, "Oh, do you have a cat?" Just once I would like to say "No, it's for company!"
- Employment application blanks always ask, "Who is to be notified in case of a emergency?" I think you should write, "A good doctor!"
- Finally, I have learned over the years that people seem to read the Bible a whole lot more as they get older. Then, it dawned on me, maybe they were cramming for their finals!

Well, are you edified yet? I don't know what more I can say except, personally, I'm hoping God grades me on the curve. However, I can't do anything about it until the finals, so why worry about it. Just to be on the safe side, I may say an extra prayer or two tonight!

Words of Wisdom a Father Could Love – June 19, 2005

To the editor:

In my past letters to the editor on Father's Day, I always tried to heap words of praise to honor the gentleman who helped guide us through life – good old Dad. He always had some very inspiring "sermons" and words of wisdom to impart and we remembered them the rest of our lives – right?

I recently read some words of wisdom or words of love from dad that brought some big smiles to my face. I wonder if today's younger generation is still getting these comments from their modern day Dads? Or, are these time honored traditions? Anyway, let's see how many you remember getting from your dad … or mother.

- Don't ask me, ask your mother.
- Close the door! Were you raised in a barn? (One of my favorites!)
- You call that a haircut?
- This will hurt me more than it hurts you.
- You call that noise "music?"
- I'm not talking just to hear my voice!
- What do you think I am, a bank?
- What did I just finish telling you?
- If I catch you doing that just one more time …!!!
- Do what your mother said!
- When I was your age …
- DON'T MAKE ME STOP THIS CAR!

Well, whatcha think? I bet you have a big smile on your face, don't you? Right, well, keep it there – that's where it belongs and that's where it will always be, if you don't sweat the little things.

Ponderings – July 9, 2005

To the editor:

It's been a long time (too long) since I've sent any "Ponderings" to your readers.

I've collected a few new ones which I would like to share with your readers. I hope everyone enjoys them as much as I did.

- Why is there a light in the fridge and not the freezer?
- If Jimmy cracks corn and no one cares, why is there a song about him?
- Can a hearse carrying a corpse drive in the carpool?
- Why does Goofy stand erect while Pluto remains on all fours? They're both dogs.
- Why do the Alphabet song and Twinkle, Twinkle Little Star have the same tune?
- Do illiterate people get the full effect of alphabet soup?
- Did you ever notice that when you blow in a dog's face, he gets mad at you, but when you take him

out for a car ride, he sticks his head out the window?

- Does pushing the elevator button more than once make it arrive faster?

Well, whatcha think? Let me close this with my final thought for the day. Live well, laugh often, don't sweat the little things and keep a smile on your face – it'll make people wonder what you've been up to.

Great Truths that Adults Have Learned – July 18, 2005

To the editor:

I submitted a letter to the editor titled, "Great truths that little children have learned."

Remember? Here are a couple of reminders: "No matter how hard you try, you can't baptize cats." "You can't hide a piece of broccoli in a glass of milk" and my favorite, "Don't wear polka-dot underwear under white shorts." Now you remember, don't you?

A good friend just forwarded me some "Great truths that adults have learned." I've included a few of my own so please enjoy:

- Raising teenagers is like nailing Jell-O to a tree.
- Wrinkles don't hurt.
- Families are like fudge … mostly sweet, with a few nuts.
- Middle age is when you choose your cereal for the fiber, not the toy.
- Your secrets are safe with your friends because they can't remember them.
- There's nothing left in your life to learn the hard way.
- Things you buy now won't wear out.
- Your joints are more accurate meteorologists than the National Weather Service.

Now that wasn't so bad, was it? Just the facts of life! Personally I like who I am and really enjoy aging. If it only didn't lead to death, it would be perfect! Oh well, that's God's responsibility so I'm not going to sweat those little things. Have a great day.

Knowing Catholicism – July 28, 2005

To the editor:

I normally try not to get involved in the political or religious discussions because both are such complicated subjects. Also, most people are opinionated, and believe they are always right. I'm not like that though – I'm open minded!

However, since there is something mystical about Catholicism I think it behooves me to divulge some of my knowledge and enlighten my non-Catholic friends. As a practicing Catholic for over 80 years, I think I am qualified to pass on some of the church's rituals and code words for your enlightenment. Here goes …

- AMEN: The only part of a prayer that everyone knows.
- BULLETIN: Your receipt for attending Mass.
- HOLY WATER: A liquid whose chemical formula is H20LY.
- INCENSE: Holy Smoke.
- JESUITS: An order of priests noted for their ability to find colleges with good basketball teams.
- JONAH: The original "JAWS" story.
- JUSTICE: When kids have kids of their own.
- MANGER: Where Mary gave birth to Jesus because Joseph wasn't covered by an HMO. (The Bible's way of showing us the holiday travel has always been rough."
- RELICS: People who have been going to Mass for so long, they actually know when to sit, kneel and stand.
- RECESSIONAL HYMN: The last song at Mass often sung a little more quietly, since most of the people have already left.

Well, how many of you are ready to convert? Or do you think you're going to need a little more enlightenment? Think about it for awhile and if you see me out and about you can stop me and ask your questions. In the meantime, don't forget to say your nightly prayers – and please put me on your prayer list. I'll also put you on my list. One final thought – our prayer list should be to ask God to help us to "not sweat the little things." Peace.

Smiling – August 12, 2005

To the editor:

Thanks to some of the readers of my letters to the editor. They occasionally send me tidbits or interesting topics for my future letters. Take the lady who recently sent me some "Tales From The Wild" that amused me and I believe they'll amuse your readers as well. These are actual comments left on Forest Service comment cards by backpackers completing wilderness camping trips. Needless to say, I couldn't resist adding a few comments of my own!

- "Tails need to be wider so people can walk while holding hands." (What's the matter, you afraid you might get lost?)
- "Trails need to be reconstructed. Please avoid building trails that go uphill." (Why not just use the downhill trails?)
- "Too many bugs and leeches and spiders and spider webs. Please spray the wilderness to rid the area of these pests." (I suggest you take a can of Raid with you the next time.)
- "Please pave the trails so they can be plowed of snow in the winter." (Why not bring a pair of skis with you the next time or else bring your own snow shovel?)
- "The coyotes made too much noise last night and kept me awake. Please silence those annoying animals." (Why don't you wear some ear plugs?)
- "A McDonalds would be nice on the trailhead." (Sure, so would a Burger King or Arby's!)
- "Need more signs to keep area pristine." (How about signs pointing to McDonald's and garbage cans?
- "The places where trails do not exist are not well marked." (Why don't you become a Trail Blazer and mark your own trails?)
- "Too many rocks in the mountains." (Why don't you throw them at the coyotes?)

Well, whatcha think? I was going to ask how could some people be so stupid when I remembered my grandkids, Jakie Joe and Jamie Lynne, once admonished me and told me I should never use the word stupid. OK guys, what if I say I think some of those people are a "few clowns short of a circus" or "a few beers short of a six-pack" or "the wheels spinning but the hamster's dead?" OK?

I'm sorry and I apologize – it's not my style to criticize and I think people can make any suggestions they want to. So, ole Papa Joe will keep quiet, with a smile on his face, a song in his heart and I promise not to sweat the little things. Think positive!

Double Meanings – September 14, 2005

To the editor:

How often do you see things and they don't make much sense or they don't come out the way you meant them to? Yeah, me too! We also see signs all over the place with doubtful or double meanings and we say to ourselves, "who in the heck wrote that?" Anyway, when we do see them, they are generally funny and entertaining. Let me give you a few examples my sweet Sally recently sent to me.

- Cocktail lounge in Norway – Ladies are requested not to have children in the bar.
- Dry cleaners, Bangkok – Drop your trousers here, for the best results.
- In a Nairobi restaurant – Customers who find our waitresses rude ought to see the manager.
- A sign on the automatic hand dryer – Do not activate with wet hands.
- In a cemetery – Persons are prevented from picking flowers from any but their own grave.
- Tokyo hotel rules and regulations – Guests are requested not to smoke or do other disgusting behaviors in bed.
- Hotel Yugoslavia – The flattening of underwear with pleasure if the job of the chambermaid.

- Hotel, Japan – You are invited to take advantage of the chambermaid.
- A sign posted in Germany's Black Forest – It is strictly forbidden on our Black Forest camping site that people of a different sex, for instance, men and women, live together in one tent unless they are married with each other for this purpose.
- A laundry in Rome – Ladies, leave your clothes here and spend the afternoon having a good time.

Can you believe that? I think most of the people who wrote those signs need to work on their language skills. Back to night class guys! Anyway, they are very entertaining and I hope you enjoyed them.

The sign in my house says, "Laugh and don't perspire the big things." Maybe it should be "Smile and don't sweat the little things." Stay happy!

Visit Someone in a Nursing Home – November 14, 2005

To the editor:

Nearly two years ago, (where does the time go? At the rate I'm going I'll be 100 before I know it.) I wrote a letter to the editor on nursing home residents and how few visits they get. "Where's the family?"

When making daily visits to see my wife, I take the time to talk to and visit as many residents as I can. There are a lot of dear sweet, lonely and lovely ladies waiting for someone to visit them.

Remember me telling you about how much happiness I got out of visiting and seeing them, especially when they gave me a smile? Also, one in particular who would extend her frail little hands to greet me?

As I would hold her delicate little hands in my left hand, I would gently put my right hand on her fragile shoulders to comfort her. She could understand me better with me speaking in her left ear.

When I patted or gently rubbed her shoulder, she would start to hum pleasant sounds of um-m-m-m. Then she would scrunch forward and murmur to me, lower, lower, lower! Agnes sure loved to have her back rubbed!

Quite frequently, as I was talking to Agnes, I would say to her, "I love you." One day she replied to me, "I love you too – I don't know what we would do without each other." She rolled her eyes at me and smiled which made me chuckle and put a BIG smile on my face. What a darling sweet lady – I'll never forget her.

No more back rubs or "I love yous" now because Agnes passed away several weeks ago at the ripe old age of 107. Agnes, you are gone but not forgotten! You have given me lots of happiness and have brightened my days on many occasions. I still think about you every time I pass your room. I still love you and miss you very, very much. I'll bet God sure was happy to see you.

Friends, if you haven't visited a loved one in a nursing home recently, please do it while you still can. Don't procrastinate, you might be too late. One of these days your loved one will be leaving to go visit Agnes.

Oh, the Good Old Days

To the editor:

Quite often we hear about the "good old days" but how much do we really know about how things were then? I don't mean 10, 30 or 70 years ago – I mean something like 500 years ago! I have discovered some very interesting facts about the 1500s that I think will help all of us have a better understanding of how it was in the "good old days."

Most people got married in June because they took their yearly bath in May, and still smelled pretty good by June. However, they were starting to smell, so brides carried a bouquet of flowers to hide the body odor. Hence the custom today of carrying a bouquet when getting married.

Baths consisted of a big tub filled with hot water. The man of the house had the privilege of the nice clean water, then all the other sons and men, then the women and finally the children. Last of all the babies. By then the water was so dirty you could actually lose someone in it. Hence the saying, "Don't throw the baby out with the bath water."

Houses had thatched roofs – thick, straw-piled high, with no wood underneath. It was the only place for animals to get warm, so all the cats and other small animals (mice, bugs) lived in the roof. When it rained it became slippery and sometimes the animals would slip and fall off the roof. Hence the saying "It's raining cats and dogs."

There was nothing to stop things from falling into the house. This posed a real problem in the bedroom where bugs and other droppings could mess up your nice clean bed. Hence, a bed with big posts and a sheet hung over the top afforded some protection. That's how canopy beds came into existence.

The floor was dirt. Only the wealthy had something other than dirt. Hence the saying "dirt poor." The wealthy had slate floors that would get slippery in the winter when wet, so they spread thresh (straw) on the floor to help keep their footing. As the winter wore on, they added more thresh until when you opened the door it would all start slipping outside. A piece of wood was placed in the entranceway. Hence the word "threshold." (Getting quite an education, aren't you?)

In those old days, bread was divided according to status. Workers got the burnt bottom of the loaf, the family got the middle, and guests got the top, or "upper crust."

Lead cups were used to drink ale or whisky. The combination would sometimes knock the imbibers out for a couple of days. Someone walking along the road would take them for dead and prepare them for burial. They were laid out on the kitchen table for a couple of days and the family would gather around and eat and drink and wait and see if they would wake up. Hence the custom of holding a "wake."

Now you know don't you – and it's all the truth. Now, whoever said history was boring?

Help for Daily News Readers Who Need to Chill Out – December 18, 2005

To the editor:

I have been down here in Naples for a few weeks and I read the letters to the editor every day. The thing I can't understand is why so many people write in and all they're doing is griping or complaining about something.

Come on people – chill out! Be thankful for all the wonderful things you have – relax and enjoy life and yourself and don't sweat all those little things!

Let me see if I can bring a little levity into your life and a smile to your face. Here's some Christian one liners I've compiled.

- Quit griping about your church. If it was perfect you couldn't belong.
- If God is your co-pilot – swap seats!
- Don't wait for six strong men to take you to church.
- If the church wants a better pastor, it only has to pray for the one it has.
- People are funny – they want the front of the bus, the middle of the road, and the back of the church.
- I don't know why some people change churches – what difference does it make which one you stay home from.

There, don't you feel better now? Like I said, "Don't sweat the little things!"

- He who dies with the most toys is none the less dead.
- Ham and eggs, a day's work for a chicken, a lifetime commitment for a pig.
- The trouble with life is there's no background music.

Here's one more for the road. "I smile because I don't know what the heck is going on!" I'm only kidding! I smile all the time because I am thankful for all that God has given me and done for me. Also, because I have so many friends – you!

So, I say unto you – keep a smile on your face, a song in your heart and be good to everyone, especially yourself, because you deserve it. And, don't sweat the little things.

Can't Be a Man – December 21, 2005

To the editor:

How many of you remember when you were first told that there was no Santa Claus? Quite a shock wasn't it? I hope you got over it because now I am going to lay an A-bomb on you!

I hate to be the one to tell you this and have to be the one to defy the sacred myth, but I truly believe "he's a she!" Santa Claus, that is! Think about it. Christmas is a big organized, warm, fuzzy, nurturing social deal and I have a hard time believing a guy could possibly pull it off.

Let me give you a few reasons why Santa can't possibly be a man.

- Men can't pack a bag.
- Men would rather be dead than caught wearing red velvet.
- Men would feel their masculinity is threatened, having to be seen with all those elves.
- Men don't answer their mail.
- Men would refuse to allow their physique to be described even in jest as anything remotely resembling a bowl full of jelly.
- Men are not interested in stockings unless somebody's wearing them.
- Having to do the Ho! Ho! Ho! Thing would seriously inhibit their ability to pick up women.
- Finally, being responsible for Christmas would require a commitment.

I can buy the fact that other mythical characters are men. Father time shows up once a year unshaven and looking ominous. Definite guy. Cupid flies around carrying weapons. Uncle Sam is a politician who likes to point fingers. Any one of those individuals could pass the testosterone screening test. But not St. Nick! Not a chance.

As long as we have each other, good will, peace on earth, faith and Nat King Cole's "Christmas", it probably makes little difference what gender Santa is. I just wish she'd quit dressing like a guy.

Marjorie Rose and I wish all of you a very Merry Christmas and a Happy New Year!

Words To Live By – January 24, 2006

To the editor:

Several years ago, a good friend of mine, "Rock," and a good friend of many of my fellow retired co-workers sent me some "Words To Live By." He still sends me or gives me advice occasionally, when he's not moving – from golf course to golf course, that is. I just found his list and would like to share it with your readers. Enjoy.

- Accept the fact that some days you're the pigeon, and some days you're the statute.
- Drive carefully. It's not only cars that can be recalled by their maker.
- Eat a live toad in the morning and nothing worse will happen to you for the rest of the day.
- If you can't be kind, at least have the decency to be vague.
- It may be that your sole purpose in life is simply serve as a warning to others.
- The early worm gets eaten by the bird, so sleep late.
- Birthdays are good for you – the more you have, the longer you live.
- Some mistakes are too much fun to make only once.
- Don't cry because it's over; smile because it happened.

Well Rock, I'm smiling because you made it happen – you sent that list to me. It also made me happy because I'm sending it on to my friends. To show my appreciation, the next time we play golf I'm going to give you those 10-inch putts. My personal words to live by? I'm going to live to be 100 – or die trying!

A happy, prosperous and healthy new year to everyone.

Yes, Children – February 3, 2006

To the editor:

What makes the world go around? Children – what else? Aren't they wonderful? To those of you have children and they get out of control, you can take comfort from the thought that even God's omnipotence did not extend to his own children.

After creating heaven and earth God created Adam and Eve and the first thing He said to them was "Don't eat the forbidden fruit!"

We all know that they did eat the fruit and God was very disappointed. His punishment was that Adam and Eve have children of their own. Thus, the pattern was set and it has never changed!

So, to your parents who have persistently and lovingly tried to give your children words of wisdom and they haven't taken them, don't be hard on yourself. If God had trouble raising children, what makes you think it would be a piece of cake for you?

Anyway, all I wanted to do was help you keep things in perspective and give you a couple of things to help you remember the good old days.

- You spend the first two years of your life teaching them to walk and talk. Then you spend the next 16 telling them to sit down and shut up.
- Grandchildren are God's reward for not killing your own children.
- Mothers of teens now know why some animals eat their young.
- Children seldom misquote you. In fact they usually repeat word for word what you shouldn't have said.
- The main reason for having children's parties is to remind you that here are children more awful than your own.
- We childproofed our home but they still got in.

Very loveable aren't they? Just remember to be nice to your kids – they will be the ones to choose your nursing home.

Don't forget the sure cure. If you have a lot of tension and you get a headache, do what it says on the aspirin bottle: "Take two aspirin and keep away from the children!"

An Encounter with Santa Claus on Christmas – December, 2005

One of the most enjoyable times of my life was visiting my grandkids during the Christmas season. One such memorable event happened during a visit to my Dallas grandkids many years ago.

We had attended a Christmas Festival and the service was fantastic. Lots of singing and caroling with all the famous Christmas songs. I can't remember ever enjoying such wonderful singing.

We came home from church, fed the kids a snack and put them to bed. Since there were so many gifts to wrap, ole Papa Joe was called on as an elf to help wrap them.

Papa Joe finally got to bed around 11:45 p.m. and as I was saying my goodnight prayers and wishing Jesus a happy birthday and thanking Him for watching over me I heard the sounds of sleigh bells and a HO! HO! HO!

Now I knew Santa was very close. It was a little after midnight when I heard some noise in the living room where the tree was. I didn't know what to do but I certainly did not want to disturb him if it was Santa, so I just stayed in bed.

After a while I didn't hear any noise so I decided to take a peek. Boy, what a sight! Santa was sitting on the floor near the fireplace eating the cookies and drinking the milk the grandkids had put out for him before going to bed. Also, one of his reindeer (I think it was Rudolph because he had a big red nose) was munching on a big carrot.

I thought I had better get back to bed and to sleep before Santa saw me. Maybe Santa would put a gift under the tree for ole Papa Joe. I have not been naughty but a very good person.

Santa did leave the kids a lot of toys and new clothes. He also left Ole Papa Joe a dozen new golf balls.

Thank you Santa Claus! Yes we must remember how hard Santa works and thank him for all those wonderful gifts he put under the Christmas tree for us.

Also, it's very thoughtful if we slip in a "happy birthday" to Jesus Christ.

Merry Christmas.

Out of the Mouths – February 15, 2006

To the editor:

A good friend of mine in Traverse City recently sent me a picture of a small child looking toward heaven with his/her eyes closed and hands folded in prayer. It was titled "Dear God." Here is what those little darlings had to say to God.

- Dear God, please put another holiday between Christmas and Easter. There is nothing good in there now. Amanda.
- Dear God, thank you for the baby brother but what I asked for was a puppy. I never asked for anything before. You can look it up. Joyce
- Dear God, is it true that my father won't get into heaven if he uses his golf words in the house? Anita
- Dear God, I like the story about Noah the best of all of them. You really made up some good ones. I like walking on water, too. Glenn
- Dear God, did you mean for Giraffes to look like that or was it an accident? Norma
- Dear God, how come you did all those miracles in the old days and don't do any now? Billy
- Dear God, maybe Cain and Able would not kill each other so much if they each had their own rooms. It works out OK with me and my brother. Larry
- Dear God, my brother told me about how we are born but it just doesn't sound right. What do you say? Marsha
- Dear God, is Father Jim a friend of yours, or do you just know him through the business? Donny
- Dear God, it's so great the way you always get the stars in the right place. Why can't you do that with the moon? Jeff
- Dear God, I am doing the best I can. Really! Papa Joe

Oops, I just had to slip that last one in! And I have been saving the best for last.

- Dear God, I didn't think orange went with purple until I saw the sunset you made on Tuesday night. That was really cool. Thomas

What can I say – except children really are so loving and adorable and wonderful. Thank you dear God for the four fantastic children you gave to Margie and me. Bless you all!!!

The Short List – March 16, 2006

To the editor:

One time I was a very avid reader, especially when I was on beach duty in Florida. Reading is not only enjoyable but also a good pastime. Ii also highly recommend it as an educational tool for children. Reading does not include Playboy!!!

Unfortunately, as much as I enjoy reading, I sometimes get so heavily involved in life's daily activities I can't find the time to read. What really irks me is when I get involved in a project, put the book aside and by the time I get back to reading it, I have forgotten part of the story. Fear not though, as I have found a solution to the problem. A short-minded friend of mine from out East has compiled a list of the world's shortest books. In case some of your readers might be interested, I am listing a few of my favorites. Sure hope you enjoy them.

- THINGS I LOVE ABOUT BILL ... by Hillary Clinton
- HOW I SERVED MY COUNTRY ... by Jane Fonda
- THINGS I CANNOT AFFORD ... by Bill Gates
- MY FAVORITE BOOK OF PERSONAL HYGIENE ... by Osama Bin laden
- A COLLECTION OF MOTIVATIONAL SPEECHES ... by Dr. J. Kevorkian
- MY PLAN TO FIND THE REAL KILLERS ... by O.J. Simpson
- GUIDE TO DATING ETIQUETTE ... by Mike Tyson

And the world's number one shortest book:

- MY BOOK OF MORALS ... by Bill Clinton with introduction by The Rev. Jesse Jackson

Well, whatcha think? I do know for certainty that since I have been reading these books, I have considerably more time for my community and service projects!! Want to buy some light bulbs? Donate a pint of blood? Make a donation in the Alzheimer's Memory Walk? Let me know if I can help you – I'm always willing to help out my friends.

In the meantime, keep a smile on your face, a song in your heart and don't sweat the little books ... oops, I mean little things!

Serving His Country on the Beaches of Florida – April 4, 2006

To the editor:

   As the old cliché goes, when things aren't going quite as well as you would like, you say, "There ain't no joy in Mudville tonight!" I'm not in Mudville, but I was in temporary puddlesville for a while. Unfortunately that nasty old disease has raised its ugly head again, but we got right after it with a little surgery. Now we wait and see!

Not to worry though, as I'm very confident my good friend Dr. Bu got all the bad stuff. I will have to start taking treatments in a month or so. All will be A-OK!

So what's new now? Do you remember a couple of months ago when I finished a series of treatments and Dr. Bu said I had a month or so before I started another series? That same week the governor of Florida contacted me and asked me if I would do some anti-terrorist surveillance work on the Gulf of Mexico beach here in Naples, Florida.

Guess what, good friends? As coincidental and unbelievable as it sounds, the governor has contacted me again, as he is still very concerned about the possibility of a terrorist attack. He said he was very impressed with my duty in the past and wants me to come back for another month's duty.

As in the past, he said my duty would be to sit on the Naples beach and be on the lookout for any foreign vessels that might attack America. I willingly accepted the challenge and told the governor I was proud to make the sacrifice for my country. I expect no pay and am only doing my patriotic duty. God bless America!

As I write this, I am happy to report that things are going quite well. My job is a little more pleasant with these warm, gentle southern breezes to help cool me down on these hot, 80+ degree days. Yes, it's not, but remember I'm doing this for my country.

As I sit on the beach gazing over the Gulf of Mexico, looking for enemy vessels, I also enjoy watching the pelicans and cormorants diving for fish. I especially enjoy the tiny sand pipers as they flit to and fro on the beach.

I hate to cut this report short, but I have to get some sleep so I'll be rested up for my shift on the beach tomorrow, when the sun comes up. This time, I'm using a 45 sunscreen to help keep my octogenarian skin from burning. I sure wouldn't want to get a bad sunburn and be injured in the line of duty. It might hamper my chances of being recognized and honored for my contributions and service to my country.

God Bless America – and Florida – and the Naples Beach! I am not sweating the little things – like sweating in the hot sun!

Papa Joe Reports from Good Ol' Midland – April 24, 2006

To the editor:

   I am happy to report that I am back home after my anti-terrorist tour of duty in Florida. However, I am somewhat disappointed in that a couple of my friends have commented about my good tan and have insinuated my tour of duty was more peaches and cream than work. How can they be so anti-American?

Sure, there were a few good days, and I did partake of some of the local vine ripened sweet tomatoes, plump and juicy strawberries and freshly squeezed orange juice, thanks to a kind and friendly neighbor. However, there were also some of those bad hair days. Let me give you an example.

One day I reached into the ice box (yes, things were somewhat primitive down there!) to get me one of those vine ripened tomatoes and my arm got too close to the container of freshly squeezed orange juice. Guess what? Yep, one container of fresh O.J. all over the kitchen floor! Wow! That's OK Papa Joe, don't sweat the little things, just go back to that kind neighbor and get some more fresh oranges – after you clean up that sticky mess all over the floor.

That same day I had a nice turkey sandwich for lunch and some pickled beets, one of my favorite snacks. A very enjoyable lunch until I went to clean off the table and accidentally tipped over the jar of red pickled beets. What a bloody red mess! Sliced beets and red pickling juice all over the table, floor and that nice white table cloth!

Two gallons of water, two rolls of paper towels and a lot of under-the-breath mumbling (No, no swearing because God was listening!) and all was clean again. Everything that is except that white table cloth which is now my favorite color – pink.

Oh, and those plump and juicy strawberries? They helped me salvage my bad hair day. I covered them with peaches and cream yogurt and ate to my heart's content. Um-m-m good!

Yes folks, I do have a nice tan which is due to sunshine – vitamin D was recommended and prescribed by my medical advisers. I have started another series of treatment since my return home and am getting some comments regarding my tan demarcation lines. (No printable comments!)

I do feel terrific, especially now that I'm back home in good old Midland with all my friends – you. I missed all of you, but all is A-OK now that I see your smiling faces again. God bless.

What Children Say About Their Mothers – May 14, 2006

To the editor:

Every year I try to pay homage to our mothers on their designated day – Mother's Day. It is always easy for us grown-ups to say many nice and wonderful things about Mothers, but what about those young elementary age school children? Well, I've been saving the following for over a year and I think it's time to share them with readers. This group of children was asked several questions about "Mothers" and here are some of their answers.

Why did God make mothers?
- She's the only one who knows where the Scotch tape is.
- Mostly to clean the house.

How did God make mothers?
- God made my mother the same, like He made me, He just used bigger parts.

What ingredients are mothers made of?
- God made mothers out of clouds and angel's hair, and everything nice in the world and one dab of mean.
- They had to get their start from men's bones. Then they mostly used string, I think.

Why did God give you your mother and not some other mom?
- God knew she liked me a lot more than other moms like me.

What kind of girl was your mom?
- I don't know because I wasn't there, but my guess would be bossy.
- They say she used to be very nice.

Why did your mom marry your dad?
- My dad makes the best spaghetti in the world. And mom eats a lot.
- My grandma says that mom didn't have on her thinking cap.

Who's the boss at your house?
- Mom. You can tell by room inspection. She sees the stuff under the bed.

What's the difference between moms and dads?
- Dads are stronger and taller but moms have all the power because that's who you have got to ask if you want to sleep over at your friend's.

If you could change one thing about your mom, what would it be?
- I would like for her to get rid of those invisible eyes on her back.
- I'd make my mom smarter. Then she would know it was my sister who did it and not me.

Out of the mouths of babes, eh? Well, one thing we all know, all mothers like to be hugged and kissed. So, this Mother's Day fortify your love and appreciation for her by giving her a big gentle hug and tender kiss. Oh, don't forget Grandma either 'cause she likes hugs and kisses just as much as mom. Besides, she's the one who lets you put your veggies back in the pot if you don't want to eat them. Remember?

My 13-year-old grandson in Texas had a school assignment where he was asked to write on "Who makes the biggest difference in your life?" His message also is appropriate for Mother's day.

By Dylan John.

The person who makes the biggest difference in my life to me would be my mom, caring and loving. She has always been there for me if I needed help getting something, feeling like she helps me more than I help her and thinking that she is the most not self-centered person I know. Seeing the exhaustion in my face, she would take me where I needed to go. If I was in trouble she would always be the one of my two parents to give me the least punishment. She has taught me the rights and wrongs of life, hard and long over the years. She has always helped me with work or projects if I didn't understand it. Whenever I'm not feeling good she is there to take care of me and get me better even if she has to work. Rain falling, she will get up and go get me supplies or a book if I need it for school or something important right away. Wonderful parent. She has made probably the biggest impact in my life. Snowing rapidly, she would always be at a football game. She always made it no matter how cold or rainy it was. My mom, self sacrificing and easy going, is the person I want to be like when I grow up.

P.S. My grandpa is Papa Joe.

It's About Love – June 1, 2006

To the editor:

This is another letter of love! On Mother's Day I submitted a letter written by my grandson Dylan John, age 13. It was an actual school assignment on "Who Makes the Biggest Difference in Your Life?" That person in Dylan's life was "My mom, caring and loving." That answer wasn't too hard to figure out, was it?

This world is full of love – if only more of us would let it come out and give more of it away. Don't be afraid or ashamed to say "I love you." Try it and see how many wonderful smiles and big hugs you'll get in return. Love comes in many ways. Let me tell you how Kaitlyn Rose, Dylan John's 16-year-old sister, expressed her love to Papa Joe during a visit last year.

During this visit, Katie would get on the computer and do all kinds of things, like get on the Internet and dozens of other things that amaze me. Anyway, I found two notes posted on my "catch all" bulletin board. (Actually, it's my dining room wall!) Anyway, here's what the notes had to say:

"Papa, you are the most inspiring person in my life. You give me the strength to wake up every morning. I love you so very much. Love, Kaitlyn.

The next was a composition and was titled: "Have faith in me."

The Lord is with you and so am I.
He is the light but I am by your side
Through thick and thin, through love and hate
I will always be there and you will always be
In my heart, in my prayers and in my soul.
You are my everything, my all and all,
You are my Papa Joe.

Well, whatcha think? Do you think Katie was trying to tell her Papa Joe that she loves him? I have five grandchildren and they are all very kind, caring and loving just like their mothers, who taught them to be like that. Their mothers are also very kind, caring and loving, and they were taught to be like that by their mother – my dear, sweet, kind and caring wife, Marjorie Rose.

Love to everyone.

Be Thankful for Having a Great Dad – June 18, 2006

To the editor:

Hi! This is Papa Joe and I'm about to write you an unusual Father's Day letter. It's unusual in that it happened about 80 years ago and it's about my father. It's not a very happy story but I'm hoping all of you, regardless of your age, will get my message.

I was the last of eight children and when I was nearly two years of age, my father deserted my mother and all of her children. I don't know any of the details and as I grew older, I didn't want to know anymore. All I know is, I don't remember anything about him except he packed up a suitcase one night and left town with another woman.

Mom, God bless her, was left to feed, clothe and support four daughters and three sons. Mom supported us by taking in laundering and ironings. That was not an easy chore back in the late '20s and early '30s. The water had to be hand pumped from a cistern or well, heated on a wood burning stove and the clothes hand washed with a scrubbing board.

Mom was the first one up in the morning and the last one to bed at night. She fed us three meals a day, what little there was of it, and we always had on clean clothes, even if they did have patches on them. Even the socks were darned!

Mom did an outstanding job raising the seven of us and not a child ever got into trouble. All kind and loving children who loved their mother. Well, I guess I have to be truthful and tell you about the time my mother said to me, "Joe, you cause me more trouble than all the other children put together!" I really wasn't a bad kid, I was just a young, inquisitive and somewhat mischievous child.

So, what's the purpose of writing this long letter praising my mother? It's still about my father, but how could I not give credit to my fantastic mother? Yes, I had a very disappointing father, not the typical kind, loving and gentle and guiding his children through life, giving them all the support they need to accomplish their goals.

This is really a reminder, but if you have a nice dad like I think you do, you don't need one. Always tell him how much you love and respect him, not only on Father's Day but every day of your life. Tell him you really appreciate everything he has done for you and show it with a few big hugs and kisses. I missed out on all of those pleasures in my life – make sure you don't.

Did you notice all of my referrals were to my father and not dad? As my youngest daughter said to me at my retirement party, "Anyone can be a father but it takes a very special person to be called 'Dad.'"

Happy Father's Day to all of you "Dads."

Ladies Wonderful – June 24, 2006

To the editor:

Two of the least used words in the English language are "thank you." I am at fault the same as everyone else but I want to make amends now by extending my personal and sincere thanks to the Central Intermediate girls softball team. Please let me explain.

As many of you know, I take my sweet wife Marjorie Rose out for a geriatric chair ride every afternoon, weather permitting. I push her back and forth on Rodd Street from the nursing home to Collins Street several times each day.

Quite often I pause on the corner of Rodd and Collins and watch the Central girls softball team playing. Evidently some of them have noticed Marge and I watching them and several times this summer they would wave to us. I always waved back, flattered that they had noticed us.

Recently Marge and I paused to watch them, but it wasn't a game or practice session – they were just standing around chatting and celebrating their last day of school.

All at once, five of the young ladies came running over toward Marge and me. They told us they had observed us watching them and thought it was nice that we did that. In appreciation, they presented Marge with three beautiful long stemmed very colorful carnations. What a very, very thoughtful gesture from someone we didn't know! We talked for about two minutes and they went back to join their buddies.

See, not all young people are trouble makers. There are many nice kids out there in the world who sometimes take the blame for a few. Anyway, I know Central turns out a lot of wonderful kids because I just met several of them. Also, I know it for a fact because my son, John, daughters Susan, Sally and Sara, are all graduates of Central and they all turned out exceptionally well.

So, to you five wonderful ladies who made my day by giving those beautiful carnations to my wife, Marjorie, I say "thanks a million" and love to you from Marge and Papa Joe.

Some Advice for the July 4th Holiday – July 2, 2006

To the editor:

The "firecracker day," July 4th, is coming up soon and I would like to pass on some words of advice to your readers. However, before I do I would also like to pass on to them some "words of wisdom," which I haven't done in awhile, just to get them in a good mood!

- How long a minute is … depends on the side of the bathroom door you're on.
- Birthdays are good for you … the more you have, the longer you live.
- Did you ever notice that the people who are late are often much jollier than the people who have to wait on them?
- Wal-Mart is lowering prices every day, how come nothing is free?
- Some mistakes are too much fun to only make once.
- A truly happy person is one who can enjoy the scenery on a detour.

Now for those words of advice. Many people will be traveling to and fro over the July 4th holiday season visiting family and friends. Unfortunately, some people have a tendency to drink and drive. Please take a few words of advice from Dean Martin, "If you drink don't drive – in fact, don't even putt!"

The advice I wanted to give is a quote and I don't even know who to credit it to. Anyway, it goes like this, "He who goes forth on the Fourth with a fifth may not come forth on the Fifth."

Jamie and Jakie, my two youngest grandkids once admonished old Papa Joe for using the word stupid. I haven't used it since, until now. So, I say unto you "If you do drink and drive, you are stupid." And that's the truth!

And to all of you nondrinker-drivers I say unto you "I hope you have an awesome, safe and sane July 4th holiday season." And that's the truth!

No traction – August 25, 2006

To the editor:

Now that I'm "older" (but I refuse to grow up!) I've really discovered many new things in my life. Like, my wild oats have turned into prunes and all bran. And, I finally got my head together but now my body is falling apart.

Maybe I could put things into a little better perspective by describing my life as if I were a car. See if you can understand or relate to this explanation. I'm sure your age bracket will be the determining factor.

If my body were a car, this is the time I would be thinking about trading it in for a newer model. I've got bumps and dents and scratches in my finish and my paint job is getting a little dull. But that's not the worst of it. My headlights are out of focus and it's especially hard to see things up close.

My traction is not as graceful as it once was, so I do slip and slide and skid and bump into things even in the best of weather. Also, my white sidewalls are stained with varicose veins. It takes me hours to reach my maximum speed (slowest, slower, and then up to slow), and my fuel burns inefficiently.

Do you think that's bad? Here's the worst of it – almost every time I sneeze, cough or sputter, either my radiator leaks or my exhaust backfires.

So friends, whatcha think? I've got nearly 82 years on this old chassis, but I still think I can get at least 100 – or I'll die trying. I'm going to continue to think young with a positive attitude. I think all of you should do the same thing. We'll give everyone a great big smile and hug as many people as we can and get away with it. At least it's worth a try!

Follow These Steps When You Are Trying to Relax – July 22, 2006

To the editor:

I think your readers will remember the letter about my granddaughter, Kaitlyn Rose, and her expressions of love for her Papa Joe with poetry. Recently my Texas Rose sent me a list of "feel good things" for my consideration.

Katie told me to read them, one at a time, then close my eyes and take a couple of seconds to think about each subject. Well, I think it proved to be very interesting and I would like to suggest that your readers try it.

So, come on folks, give it a try. You're probably sitting there trying to relax after "a hard day at the office" and I want to help. Remember, one subject at a time, close your eyes and let your imagination run wild for at least 10 seconds. Here we go with a few subjects:

- Playing with a new puppy.
- Hearing your favorite song on the radio.
- Lying in bed listening to the rain.
- Running through sprinklers.
- Waking up and realizing you still have a few hours to sleep.
- Taking a bubble bath.

Well, what did you think? Kind of relaxing wasn't it? Kaitlyn ended her note with this quote: "Friends are great angels who lift us to our feet when our wings have trouble remembering how to fly."

Yes, we all have to be reminded from time to time about how good our lives are. I hope you all enjoyed these "natural highs" and they gave you a warm fuzzy feeling and bought a smile to your face. One final quote from me: "Smile, God loves you."

Omelets with a Zip – August 16, 2007

To the editor:

Guess what? I experienced something new on a recent visit to my daughter Sally's that I think is pretty neat and thought I would pass it on to readers for a "go at it."

An old friend sent me an e-mail describing how to make a "Ziploc Omelet." He said it works great and was especially good for when all the family is together. He was right.

During that visit to my daughter's, I volunteered to fix breakfast one morning, and it seemed that everyone wanted an omelet or scrambled eggs, but everyone wanted different things in their omelets. Ah ha, Papa Joe, now is the time to try those Ziploc Omelets you heard about. OK folks, here we go – get out your pad and pencil and Ziploc bags.

ZIPLOC OMELET

Have each person write his or her name on a quart Ziploc freezer bag with a permanent marker.

Crack two eggs (large or extra large) into the bag. (No more than 2.) Shake to combine them.

Put a variety of ingredients such as cheeses, ham, onions, green peppers, mushrooms, tomatoes, hash browns, salsa, etc., whatever you like in your omelet.

Each guest adds the prepared ingredients of their choice to their bag and shakes well. Then make sure the air is out of the bag and zip it up.

Place the bags into rolling, boiling water for exactly 13 minutes. You can usually cook 6-8 omelets in a large pot. For more, make another pot of boiling water.

Now, while the omelets are cooking, have people set the table, cut up some fresh fruit, make some toast, or whatever to get everyone involved in the process.

When the 13 minutes are up, carefully remove the bags from the boiling water, open them up and the omelet will roll out easily onto your plate. Salt and pepper and start to eat as everyone expresses their amazement and delight. Hmmmmm good.

Since you are probably so mesmerized by this recipe, you overlooked some of the benefits. First of all, the best part of this process is that no one has to wait for their special omelet. They get to eat what they wanted and if they don't like it, tough luck, they eat their own mistakes. The best part of all? There is no dirty stove or messy skillets to wash. My final comment, bon appétit.

Some Thoughts About the Benefits of Being a Grandparent – October 8, 2006

Since I never really knew my grandparents because they lived so far away, I never paid much attention as to when Grandparents Day was. I kind of thought it was Sept. 24, but I read the other day where the first Sunday after Labor Day isn't just a day set aside to mourn the end of summer, but a day set aside to honor grandparents. So why don't we do it now? Better late than never! Here are a few comments, quotes and proverbs I've accumulated. Hope you enjoy them.

- My grandkids believe I'm the oldest thing in the world. After two or three hours with them, I believe it, too.
- An hour with your grandchildren can make you feel young again. Anything longer than that, and you start to age quickly.
- Never have children, only grandchildren.
- My grandmother is over 80 and still doesn't need glasses. She drinks right out of the bottle.
- Grandchildren are God's way of compensating us for growing old.
- Nobody can do for little children what grandparents do. Grandparents sort of sprinkle stardust over the lives of little children.
- Grandchildren don't make a man feel old; it's the knowledge that he's married to a grandmother.
- Grandmas are moms with lots of frosting.
- It's amazing how grandparents seem so young once you become one.
- A grandparent is old on the outside but young on the inside.
- Grandmas never run out of hugs or cookies.
- Grandmas hold our tiny hands for just a little while, but our hearts forever.

A couple of years ago, I told your readers a grandma story that I would like to repeat now, just in case they missed it before.

A teacher told her first grade class to put their hands over their hearts. Lil' Joe put his hand on his fanny. The teacher said, "That's not your heart, Joe." "Yes it is, teacher, because every time my grandma picks me up, she pats me there and says, 'Bless your little heart, Joe.'"

Love to all of you grandparents – from the bottom of my heart!

One Day at a Time – November 12, 2006

To the editor:

One of my many philosophies is to take life "one day at a time." Remember? Yesterday is history, tomorrow is a mystery, but today is the present – a gift from God! It's like every day is your birthday – you get the gift of life every day.

Let me tell you a story I read about an elderly, well-poised and proud man who is fully dressed each morning by eight o'clock, with his hair fashionably combed and shaved perfectly, even though he is legally blind.

His wife had passed away several months ago, making it necessary to move into a nursing home. As he was maneuvering his way to the elevator and being ushered to his new home, the administrator was providing him with a visual description of his tiny room. "I love it," he said. "Mr. Jones, you haven't seen the room yet – just wait."

"That doesn't have anything to do with it," he replied. "Happiness is something you decide on ahead of time. Whether I like the room or not doesn't depend on how the furniture is arranged – it's how I arrange it in my mind. I have already decided to love it. It's like a decision I make every morning when I wake up. I have a choice – I can spend the day in bed recounting the difficulty I have with the parts of my body that no longer work or get out of bed and be thankful for the ones that do."

What a wonderful example for all of us, eh? Each day is a gift from God and we should focus on all the happy memories we have stored away in our minds. I am learning that old age is like a bank account. You can withdraw from it what you have put in it. So my advice to all of you would be to deposit a lot of happiness in your bank of memories for future withdrawals.

I would also suggest you start today because if you don't, you are losing some of the happiest times in your life for future reference. Think positive and, please, don't sweat the little things. May God smile on you today – and tomorrow – and the next day.

An Inspiration – November 25, 2006

To the editor:

Thanks to the City of Midland Beautification Advisory Committee for a lifetime experience of gratification. I was just recently selected to receive a 2006 Appreciation of Beautification Award for Residential Landscaping, my second such award in nine years. The award was presented to me at the City Council chambers.

When asked how I have managed to beautify my yard, the answer is this: "my sweet wife, Marjorie Rose." Besides being a dedicated registered nurse for many years, Margie was very color coordinated and an excellent artist. For many years, Marge would buy the flowers and plants and say, "Joe, plant these here, those there, etc., etc." Marge was the landscaping artist; Joe was the helper or hole digger.

Unfortunately, Margie has been retired to a nursing home for the past five years with that dreadful and horrible Alzheimer's disease. As a result, I am now the landscaper (?) and still the hole digger, and Margie is a spiritual helper.

So, I attribute the beauty of my garden to my sweet Marjorie Rose who has been my life's inspiration for the past 56 years. Now that Margie can't tell me where to "plant these here and those there," I ask myself, "Joe, where would Margie like 'these and those' planted?" Then I dig a hole and plant them!

Sound stupid? Guess what? Margie has to be looking over my shoulder in spirit and giving me guidance because the system is working! I won the Beautification Award, didn't I? Thanks for your help, Margie, and don't forget, I love you.

Cheesh! – November 30, 2006

To the editor:

The other day as I was rifling (no not shot gunning) through my old files looking for a picture of me and my pet duck, Goo Goo, I found a very interesting story that I'm sure readers will enjoy.

Almost everyone knows where the hamburger originated, but not many people know how the cheeseburger was discovered.

Legend has it that a man named Hamilton Burger was once grinding sausage in his kitchen just outside Nice, France (that's pronounced neese, not nice) when he accidentally fed some lean beef into the grinder. Noting his mistake, he put the ground beef on a shallow plate and stored it in his cooler.

Later, he returned to find a large wheel of cheese had slipped from the shelf above and compressed the beef into a patty, which he named after his half sister Patricia, who married Lord Melt.

That evening, Ham, as his friends called him, put the patty in a skillet and cooked it. Surprisingly, a large piece of cheese had broken off and landed on the beef. As it cooked, the cheese melted over the patty. When Ham saw what happened, he exclaimed, "Cheesh!"

Just then, a handsome young delivery man from the newly-formed Nice Bun and Roll Co. (Yes, that's nice and not neese!) knocked on the door, offering samples of his products. When Patty saw him, she shouted "Nice Buns."

Well, the rest is history. Ham Burger and Patty Melt had invented a remarkable new food sensation … The Cheesh! Burger.

Now, wasn't that a very nice (nice!) story? Wow! I even got a little hungry writing about it so I think I'll close and go out and have a hot dog and a bowl of chili.

Ciao! That's chow!

P.S. If anyone is interested in hearing the story about Goo Goo, my pet duck, please let me know.

<u>Just for Today – January 5, 2007</u>

To the editor:

In several of my past letters to the editor, I have often talked about my philosophies of life and I always thought one of the most important ones was to "take and live life one day at a time."

Thirty-plus years ago I came into possession of a talk that was given at Cobo Hall in Detroit titled "Just For Today." I think we have all seen or heard comments pertaining to the same philosophy of life but I would like to remind you of a couple you may not have given too much thought to.

- Just for today, I will be happy. This assumes that what Abraham Lincoln said is true, that, "Most folks are about as happy as they make up their minds to be."
- Just for today, I will adjust myself to what is and not try to adjust everything to my own desires. I will take my family, my job, and my luck as they come and fit myself to them.
- Just for today, I will take care of my body. I will exercise it, care for it and nourish it and not abuse or neglect it.
- Just for today, I will try to strengthen my mind. I will try to learn something that requires effort, thought and concentration.
- Just for today, I will be agreeable. I will look as well as Ii can, dress as becoming as possible, talk low, act courteous, be liberal with praise and not criticize or find fault with anything, and not try to regulate or improve anyone.
- Just for today, I will have a quiet half-hour, all by myself, and relax. In this half-hour, sometime, I will think of spiritual things, so as to get a little more perspective to my life.
- Just for today, I will be unafraid, especially, I will not be afraid to be happy, to enjoy what is beautiful, to love and to believe that those I love, love me.
- Just for today, I will make decisions as wisely as possible, then forget it. The moment of absolute certainty never arrives.
- Just for today, I will try to live this day only –not tackle my whole life problems at once.
- Just for today, I will be my best self. I will dare to be different and to follow my own star. Just for today!

Well, whatcha think? Boy, there sure are a lot of things to remember day after day, isn't there? Now we have a few reminders. Let's think of them as New Year's resolutions, starting today, just for today. Maybe if we take them one day at a time they may get repetitious and the first thing we know, we'll be living for today, every day. Does that make any sense? Let's try it and see how it enriches our lives!

May God smile on you today.

<u>**So Soon? – January 10, 2007**</u>

To the editor:

"Joe, what are you doing back home from Florida so soon?" Several people asked me that question recently after my return from Florida. Gosh, it's nice to know that people knew I was gone and missed me. Thanks to all of you for thinking about me.

Yes, I recently returned from my anti-terrorist tour of duty in Naples and all went very well, thank you. Fortunately (?), the weather was cold, cloudy and windy and the Gulf was very choppy so those darn terrorists couldn't get anywhere near our shores. Yes, it didn't make my tour very pleasant but that was the sacrifice I was making for my country.

Unfortunately, due to those cold and cloudy days, I was not able to get enough sunshine vitamin D that I needed for my health. Now I probably will have to go back for another tour and get my needed supply of sunshine. Oh well, anything for my country – God bless America! I will keep you posted.

I do have to tell you one humorous thing that happened one day while I was patrolling the beach for invaders. I was walking along the water's edge – me and the gulls and the sandpipers – when I glanced toward the shore and saw a very large beach umbrella tumbling down the beach at a high rate of speed and a man chasing it.

Every once in a while the umbrella would slow down its journey and as the man chasing it got a little closer, the wind would pick up and it would take off again at a greater rate of speed. Needless to say, quite a few bystanders were taking this all in with a great deal of amusement.

The man in pursuit finally caught up with his umbrella and as he was collapsing it to take back to its original place on the beach, all of the bystanders who had been observing the episode started applauding and yelling "bravo." I don't think the man was very pleased with our action and comment, but we were having an enjoyable time. I once read a quote that said, "When the wind blows, go with it." That's all the umbrella was doing! That man has got to learn "not to sweat the little things."

Kids Say the Darndest Things – January 22, 2007

To the editor:

I have written many letters to the editor, but I think the ones I have enjoyed the most are the ones about small children – and their comments. Sweet, pure, inexperienced innocence. You gotta love the way kids think, don't you? Here's a few I picked up last year.

JACK, 3, was watching his Mom breastfeeding his new baby sister. After awhile he asked: "Mom, why have you got two? Is one for hot and one for cold milk?"

MELANIE, 7, asked her Grannie how old she was. Grannie said she didn't remember anymore. Said Melanie, "If you don't remember, you should look in the back of your pantsies. Mine say five to six."

STEVEN, 5, hugged and kissed his Mom goodnight. "I love you so much that when you die I'm going to bury you outside my bedroom window."

BRITTANY, 6, had an earache and wanted a pain killer. She tried in vain to take the lid off the bottle. Seeing her frustration, her Mom explained it was a childproof cap and she'd have to open it for her. Eyes, wide with wonder, the little girl asked, "How does it know it's me?"

SUSAN, 5, was drinking juice when she got the hiccups. Please don't give me this juice again," she said. "It makes my teeth cough."

DIANE, 4, stepped on the bathroom scale and asked, "How much do I cost?"

MARC, 5, was engrossed in a young couple that were hugging and kissing in a restaurant. Without taking his eyes off them, he asked his dad: "Why is he whispering in her mouth?"

CLINTON, 5, was in his bedroom looking worried. When Mom asked what was troubling him, he replied, "I don't know what'll happen with this bed when I get married. How will my wife fit in?"

JAMES, 5, was listening to a Bible story. His dad read, "The man named Lot was warned to take his wife and flee out of the city, but his wife looked back and was turned to salt." Concerned, James aside, "What happened to the flea?"

TAMMY, 6, was with her mother when they met an elderly, rather wrinkled woman her mom knew. Tammy looked at her for awhile and then asked, "Why doesn't your skin fit your face?"

And, the Sunday sermon this Mom will never forget: "Dear Lord," the minister began, with arms extended toward heaven and a rapturous look on his upturned face. "Without you, we are but dust." He would have continued, but at that moment the woman's very obedient daughter – who was listening – leaned over to her mother and asked quite audibly in her shrill little girl voice, "Mom, what is butt dust?"

Every time I write about children and their quotes, I always finish my letters with "What more can I say?" So, "What more can I say?" Except, thank you God for giving us those wonderful little pieces of joy and love!

Hugs to Spare – February 3, 2007

To the editor:

The other day I saw a note in my Month-at-a-Glance calendar (a must in my life!) that Huggers Day was in January. I don't think I ever did know what the exact date was but I don't really think it's important – every day should be Huggers Day.

The reason I mention this is that the other day I found a "hugs" card from my dear, sweet daughter Sally, which reminded me of Huggers Day.

"Hugs can tell you it's OK to be yourself. Hugs can tease you out of your too serious moments. Hugs can show someone's listening – even when you're not making any sense. Hugs can comfort your little kid needs and give you hope that things will all be better someday soon. Hugs can let you know there's someone you can count on in this crazy world."

Then Sally's personal note, "Sending you a little hug with lots of love." Then her love note, "I love you once ... I love you twice ... I love you more than beans 'n' rice. Hugs from me to you. Love, Sally."

Very nice, eh? I don't know if Sally loves beans and rice that much, but I do know that when she says that, you have received the highest compliment in the world!

The point I'm trying to make is, regardless of the exact date, every day should be Huggers Day. Every day! I doubt if any of you can remember my letter to the editor dated 11-10-02 titled "Take the time to give someone a hug today." That letter was prompted by a book my youngest daughter, Sara, sent to me 25 years ago. It was titled "The Hug Therapy Book." That book changed my life – I've been thinking and giving hugs ever since.

In that letter, I was advocating and promoting hugging. I still do, every day of my life and without all those hugs I wouldn't be so happy.

Thanks God!

So I am reminding you today, as I did nearly five years ago, "Who is the nearest person to you as you read this letter? OK, now get up and slowly walk over to that person, slim or tall, large or small, and say 'I need a nice hug, how about you?'"

Well, how did you make out? I'll bet you a hug you got one, didn't you? And didn't it give you a nice, warm fuzzy feeling? You betcha! What a life, eh?

Finally, as I told you five years ago, if you see ol' Papa Joe out and about and you need a hug, I will be more than happy to oblige you. I can never get enough hugs!

My motto for today is, "Never wait until tomorrow to hug someone you could hug today, because when you give one, you get one right back your way."

May God bless all of you.

What is Love? – February 25, 2007

To the editor:

What does love mean? I know I can go to the dictionary and get an explanation but that still doesn't answer my question. I know what love is by the feel of it but I can't describe or explain it. I'm going to dwell into this subject and I promise you an answer in the future. I hope!

In the meantime, what do you do when you want an answer to a delicate question? You go to the young uninhibited children. I recently read when a group of professional people asked a group of young children, "What does love mean?", their answers were broad and deeper than anyone could imagine. See what you think:

- Love is what makes you smile when you're tired.
- Love is when you kiss all the time. Then when you get tired of kissing, you still want to be together and talk more. My Mom and Dad are like that. They look gross when they kiss.
- Love is when Mommy sees Daddy all dirty and smelly and says he's still handsomer than Robert Redford.
- Love is when your puppy licks your face even after you left him alone all day.
- I know my older sister loves me because she gives me all of her old clothes and has to go out and buy new ones.
- When you love somebody, your eyelashes go up and down and little stars come out of you.
- Love is when Mommy sees Daddy on the toilet and she doesn't think it's gross.

Papa Joe says you really shouldn't say "I love you" unless you mean it. But if you mean it, you should say it a lot. Sometimes people forget!

One final story to wrap this up. Author and lecturer Leo Buscaglia once talked about a contest he was asked to judge. The purpose of the contest was to find the most caring child. The winner was a four-year-old child whose next door neighbor was an elderly gentleman who had recently lost his wife. Upon seeing the man cry, the little boy went into the old gentleman's yard, climbed onto his lap, and just sat there. When his mother asked what he had said to the neighbor, the little boy said, "Nothing, I just helped him cry."

That's what love means.

Community is Wonderful – February 10, 2007

To the editor:

I hope I can adequately express my most sincere thanks and appreciation to everyone who came to see my family and I in our recent time of need. Our dear, sweet Marjorie Rose, wife, mother and grandmother, was recently taken to heaven by God almighty to be with him and Margie's heaven family. Margie has had a very long journey in this life and deserves to be with God and her family. Margie is now at peace.

I apologize for not being able to spend more personal time with each of you who came to pay respects to Margie, but there were too many of you, with lots of fond memories of the "good old days," but so little time to reminisce. Please keep those fond memories of Marjorie in your heart.

My family and I want to sincerely thank all of you who sent so many beautiful flowers and plants. I am also deeply appreciative of the numerous donations so many of you gave in Margie's memory to the Alzheimer's Association and the Midland Lions Club charities. I'm sure they will be very grateful and the gifts will assist them in their efforts to make lives better and this world a better place to live in.

We cannot forget to thank those of you who brought or sent food to our family at home. We all ate very heartedly and fulfillingly! Daughter Sally took a few "doggie bags" to her home here in Michigan. Unfortunately son John and daughter Sara and her family couldn't take any on their plane rides back home to Florida and Texas. Thankfully, that left a few "doggie bags" for Papa Joe to enjoy over the next several weeks.

I am sure I have neglected to say and include everything in this letter of "thanks" so I guess the only way I can circumvent that is to say "The Lubbehusen family sends our sincere thanks and appreciation to each and every one of you for everything!" My sweet Marjorie would have been very pleased with everything you did in her honor and memory.

My family and I send our love and best wishes to all of you and we will ask God to bless all of you, keep you in good health and especially, keep you in the palm of his hand forever and ever.

Papa Joe Answers the Question, "God, why Not Me?" – May 6, 2007

God, why not me?

Many times when I visited my dear sweet Marjorie Rose in the nursing home, before she passed away, I would look at her lying there in her bed, unable to move, smile or talk. Nothing! What a shame to look at that once lovely and vivacious lady in the vegetative state, unable to do anything, the victim of that devastating Alzheimer's disease.

Frequently I would question God on why he did that to Margie, who was always kind and caring as a mother of her four beautiful children and a wonderful loving wife of 56 years. Why, God? She never did anything wrong in her entire life – she does not deserve this horrible life which has encapsulated her for so many years.

Why not me instead? I never did live up to the highest standards of life that Margie did. I know Margie would have taken extra special care of me as I did for her. I did give Margie all the love I could each time I visited her, but hers would have been a more gentle and tender mother's type of love.

Then one day I came to the realization that my present life and lifestyle was much better than it had ever been since Margie's illness. God had already made Margie a wonderful, kind and loving wife and mother so now it was time to start working on Papa Joe.

I suddenly realized that on a daily basis I now went out of my way to be good, kind and caring to everyone I met. Everyone! I gave the little kids Tootsie Rolls or candy suckers, depending on their age and mothers' approval. It's amazing how a little piece of candy can stop a child from crying and put a smile on the mother's face. And mine!

When I visited the nursing home, I had to put an extra handful of candy in my pocket. One for the receptionist, one for each of the available kitchen staff, one for the laundry lady, one for the janitorial lady, one each for the nurses or aides and always one for the residents I encountered – once I found out it was OK for individual residents to have a piece of candy.

I always got several smiles for each piece of candy I gave away. The kids, though, gave me the biggest and sweetest smiles. I smiled and tried to talk to everyone I came in contact with at the malls and in the stores – especially the employees, who needed a smile or an uplifting.

I spent as much time as I could with the residents of the nursing home. They always smiled and were always happy to see me. I never could understand why, but they don't get too many visitors. What a shame.

Then there were my many letters to the editor, always with as much humor as I could muster or an upbeat philosophical dissertation on life. "Live your life one day at a time with a positive attitude, don't sweat the little things and be thankful for everything God has given you."

Can you believe my happiness and enjoyment when people walk up to me and ask, "Aren't you Papa Joe? I just love all of your articles in the paper, please keep on writing them!" Here I am trying to make people happy and they are showering me with kindness instead. What did I really do to deserve their kindness, praise and love?

Why did I receive over 200 "get well" cards after I had cancer surgery? Or over 250 sympathy cards after my sweet Marjorie Rose passed away? They weren't just "I'm sorry" cards but pages of written testimony on how people perceived my love for my wife and everyone I encountered in my life.

Why, oh why did all those people shower that love on me? I'm no one special, just an old octogenarian trying to live my life one day at a time, with a good positive attitude and a smile on my face. And, trying to be friendly to everyone I encounter.

I am now living a new life and my future life is all planned. Let me see if I can explain it to you as Jesus explained it to his disciples many years ago. I now have my answer to "God, why not me?"

In one of his parables he portrays himself as someone on our side pulling for us. He's the gardener who tells the master not to cut down the fig tree just yet because it was not bearing fruit. He promises he will work with it and see if it might bear fruit again. He tries to get some extra time for the fig tree. But, even if the gardener succeeds in getting an extra year for the tree, it's still living on borrowed time!

We're all going to die one way or another and in perspective of the long sweep of history we're all going to die relatively soon. We are all created by God and put here on earth for a purpose. We may not know, on this side of the grave, what our purpose is, but if we do our best, in the circumstances of our own life, and live as Jesus taught us to live, we will accomplish our purpose.

I now know what I do in my life will not seem all that important, and it won't make me famous, but then I think, there is no greater nor important accomplishment than simply to do what God put me here on earth to do.

Too often, we don't take that seriously. We don't think we're that important or good. But then I realized that God has put me here to accomplish something that no one else is given to accomplish.

God put me on this earth to give Tootsie Rolls to little kids and all the other nice people I meet on a daily basis. If I don't do it, who else is going to do it?

Who else is going to talk to, sing to or give out all those "Hi, how are yous" to all those store clerks, waitresses and everyone else I encounter during my wonderful journey through life?

Who else is going to write all those letters to the editor on just about any humorous or philosophical subject, but always amusing enough that people want me to "keep on writing them."

Yes, I now know the answer to "God, why not me?" God put me down here on earth to help people enjoy life. So, folks, I guess you're stuck with me and will have to put up with my Tootsie Rolls, laughs, jokes, smiles, letters to the editor and anything else I can do to make you smile and be happy.

I'm doing the things God wants me to do on this earth. When my time runs out, I'm sure he has plans for me in my next life. In the meantime, keep a smile on your face, a song in your heart and be good to everyone, especially yourself, because you deserve it. Above all, remember Papa Joe loves you.

Lesson About Laundry – April 29, 2007

To the editor:

Hello, dear friends! Papa Joe is back home in Midland after his 10th annual snowbird blood drive in Naples and anti-terrorist surveillance work for Charlie Crist (the governor of Florida for the benefit of those of you who may not know him).

Just in case you missed the results to the snowbird blood drive, we registered 364 individuals, we had 57 first time donors and collected a fantastic 318 units of blood. That's 40 gallons of blood, which will save a lot of lives.

Incidentally, I got up to 20 gallons donated before I got cancer and couldn't donate any longer. I'm still looking for someone to carry on for me. Why don't you roll up your sleeves and go donate a pint for me. Tell 'em Papa Joe sent you!

My anti-terrorism surveillance duty went very well. You didn't hear or read about any of those foreign devils making it ashore when I was down in Naples, did you? Dedication and vigilance on my part to help protect my country! God bless America!

Now for the unfortunate incident I had while in Naples. There are a lot of "Beach People" down there – they own those multimillion dollar homes and up!

Most of those "BPs" sit up there on their verandahs, or whatever, sipping on a cocktail or two and enjoy the ships at sea and all the other beautiful scenery. I think they also occasionally look down at the Beach Bums "BBs" and observe our activities.

One day a nice lady approached me and after exchanging a few pleasantries, asked me when and how I washed my clothing. (I guess the wind must have been blowing in her direction that day!) When I was too embarrassed to answer, she told me she had some laundry faculties in her guest house and she would make them available to me if I wanted to use them.

Needless to say, I gathered all my clothing and headed for the barn – I mean the laundry room. I pretty much threw all my clothing in the washer with some soap and let her go. When I returned about 45 minutes later to put my clothes in the dryer, I noticed a noticeable bulge in the rear pocket of a pair of my shorts.

"Flashback – 1939"

I was preparing to enter the seminary and study for the priesthood, but before I left, my mother gave me my first pocket wallet. A prince gardener top grain cowhide wallet. Probably worth 25 cents in those days!

I carried that wallet with pride all my life, even during the three years I served in Europe during World War II. Yes, that wallet was worn and torn and had holes on the sides and ends from the wear and tear, but it was my first wallet and was given to me by my mother.

"Fast forward – March 2007"

Yes, that lump or bulge in my shorts pocket was the same wallet my mother gave me 68 years ago in 1939. And yes, it was a "little wet," but I removed the entire contents and managed to dry everything to the best of my ability and the situation.

I saved everything, including a picture of my dear sweet Marjorie Rose, which I have carried in that wallet since she gave it to me in 1949, the year before we were married. Not to worry though, it didn't get too wet because it was a picture of Margie in a bathing suit!

Well folks I am getting a little nostalgic and emotional just thinking about my near catastrophic accident, so I think I will close this letter and go upstairs and look at an enlarged picture of Margie in her bathing suit – just for a pick me up!

Just one other thing, the next time you do your laundry, don't forget to check the pockets for your wallet!!

God loves you and so do I.

Message to Graduates – May 25, 2007

To the editor:

Another big event in Papa Joe's life. My first grandchild, Kaitlyn Rose, my Texas beauty, will soon be graduating from high school and moving onward and upward in the academic world.

Needless to say, Katie is a highly intelligent and sophisticated lady (no, Ii am not prejudice – at least not much), but we all can use a little more advice from time to time.

While visiting my daughter, Sally, on Mother's Day, I noticed she had a list of words of wisdom on her bulletin board in the kitchen. I'm sure these words are worthwhile to send to Katie and any other high school graduate who might want to consider this wisdom. P.S. Sally is a high school teacher! Here goes:

- Life is not fair – get used to it!
- If you mess up, it's not your parents' fault, so don't whine about your mistakes, learn from them.
- Life is not divided into semesters. You don't get summers off and very few employers are interested in helping you find yourself. Do that on your own time.
- Television is not real life. In real life people actually leave the coffee shop and go to jobs.
- Be nice to nerds. Chances are you'll end up working for one.
- Before you were born, your parents weren't as boring as they are now. They got that way from paying your bills, cleaning your clothes and listening to you talk about how cool you thought you were. So before you save that rain forest from the parasites of your parents' generation, try delousing the closet in your own room!

There's some food for thought for all your grads! My sincere congratulations, good luck and I wish Kaitlyn Rose and all the other high school graduates lots of success in your journey through life – whatever it might be.

Thinking of Streaking

To the editor:

The other morning as I was laying in bed at 4:00 a.m. (I was awake because I couldn't saw anymore logs) I decided I might as well get up, make myself a cup of hot tea, relax and then go back later and saw some more logs.

While up I decided to look through an old folder of trivia. When I say old, I mean old as some of the stuff as dated 1970. It didn't take me long to get a few smiles on my face at 4 a.m. and what specifically did it was some old graffiti and streaking remarks I found.

It's not 4:00 a.m. but I'm sure I can take your readers back 35-40 years and put some big smiles on their faces. Here's a few graffiti to get them started.

- Lady Godiva rode on the wrong side of the street.
- Garbage is a collector's item.
- California deserves a fair shake.
- Headaches are all in the mind.
- Do grouchy hippies smoke crab grass?
- Lenin's grave was a communistic plot.
- Porky Pig is a boar.

Now, how about a little streaking? Streaking is nothing new, even 40 years ago. It dates back to biblical times and is verified in the New Testament. "And a certain young man followed with him, having a linen cloth cast about him, over his naked body; and they laid hold on him: but he left the linen cloth and fled naked." (I bet your readers are really surprised that Papa Joe knows so much, aren't you?)

Now, back to streaking – here's a couple of Papa Joe's favorites. Enjoy!!!

- Streaking is over baring.
- Streakers repent – your end is in sight.
- A streaker is someone unsuited for his work.
- Get closer to nature – streak the zoo.

- Streaking puts color in your cheeks.
- Streakers tan more evenly.
- Don't get too excited about the streaking fad – it's really only a passing fanny.

Well, there you are kids, hope you enjoyed this little dissertation of the good ole days. Just one question – If a streaker streaks so fast that on one sees anything but a streak, is streaking obscene?

Keep on smiling. God loves you.

All Hail Geezers – August 2, 2007

To the editor:

How many times have some of you older gentlemen been called an old fuddy duddy or old geezer? Personally, I prefer to be referred to as a sexy old senior citizen. What's wrong with the younger generation who refer to us by those names?

In believe that as I age, I get wiser and by the time I am 100 I'm going to be a very wise old man. Old age is not the years in your life, but the life in your years. I especially like the old English proverb that says, "The older the fiddler, the sweeter the tune." Truer words were never spoken!

Getting back to that slang "geezer" for us oldies, Mort Crim once gave a dissertation and a definition of what a geezer really is. Listen up!

Geezers are easy to spot. At sporting events, during our national anthem, they hold their caps over their hearts and sing without embarrassment. They know the words and believe in them. They remember the Depression, World War II, Pearl Harbor, Normandy and Hitler. They remember the atomic age, the moon landing and Vietnam.

If you bump into a geezer on the sidewalk, he'll apologize. Pass a geezer on the street and he'll nod and tip his hat to a lady. Geezers trust strangers and are courtly to women.

Geezers are embarrassed when someone curses in front of women and children.

They don't like violence or filth on TV and in movies. Geezers have moral courage. And they seldom brag, unless it's about the grandkids in Little League or at musical recitals.

In summation, I would like to say that now, more than ever, we need the thoughtfulness and the wisdom of our older citizens. You see, geezers know what it is that truly makes our nation great. I am very proud to be a geezer!

Papa Joe's Message to Grandchildren: God Loves All of You

To the editor:

In January 1993 I started writing a journal to my grandchildren entitled "PAPA JOE, A letter of Love to My Grandkids." I wrote in that journal very regularly until my wife's Alzheimer's disease steadily increased and I spent most of my time taking care of her instead of writing.

My writings were factual, humorous, educational, philosophical and anything else that would pop up in my mind. I have over 300 typewritten pages and 3-4 secretarial pads that have not been typed. Someday when I retire (???) I hope to put it all together and publish a book or two. (Know any typists or publishers?)

Recently I was looking over my notes and found a dissertation I wrote to the grandkids several years ago. It was about "Is there really a God or is it all a hoax?" Let me tell you what I told them?

"I frequently talk to God about everything under the sun. I talk to God in the morning when I get up; when I'm walking the beach; when I take my afternoon nap and when I go to bed at night. I talk to Him any time of the day or night. Sometimes I wonder if I'm bothering Him too much!

"One night I was lying in bed after saying my prayers and I started thinking about all the not-so-good things in my life – no father, a man who deserted his family; a lovely 23-year-old daughter killed in an automobile accident; a wife with that dreaded Alzheimer's disease that eventually took her life.

"Needless to say my mind was a little confused as I weighed the pros and cons of my thoughts. Then I said something to myself that I had never even thought of before. 'If there really is a God, why doesn't He give me a sign of some kind so I will really know and truly believe?' Then I drifted off to sleep.

"The next morning I started my regular routine – get my wife up and dressed, make us a cup of hot tea and then adjourn to the 'library' with the front page of the local paper. I usually start reading the front page but this morning I decided to skip to the second page and check out the lottery winners. I started turning the page, repeating to myself the numbers I always play. When I had repeated the last number, my eyes caught the winning lottery numbers. My immediate outburst heard blocks away was 'Holy mackerel!'

"Yes, I won, but my small fortune didn't last very long. The Lottery Office took Uncle Sam's share right off the top; I had to take all my friends out to celebrate; I gave the kids and grandkids a few dollars and then Papa Joe was poor again! In fact I was poorer than when I started. Why? When I got back home and filed my Michigan taxes, the governor of Michigan wanted a share of my loot, etc., etc.

"Oh well, like they say, 'Easy come, easy go.' Anyway, it was better to have won and then lost instead of not winning at all. I think! Anyway, thanks for the ride God! It was nice to be a winner for a while.

"OK kids, let me ask you a question. Was that plain old good luck that I won the lottery or was it God giving me a sign? Whatcha think? You think about it and come to your own conclusion.

"As for me, I have never ever had a doubt that there is a God! Sometimes we may want to question God, but we know He does everything, good or bad, for a reason. He would never hurt us because He loves all of us. I doubt if God was giving me a sign, but I don't care because I never did doubt Him, and He knows it. I also know that he loves me just as much now that I'm poor again. Maybe if I didn't play the lottery anymore and saved my money, then I could be reach.

"So, come on dear grandkids, put a smile on your face because there is a God, and He loves all of you!"\

It's Papa Joe – July 18, 2007

To the editor:

Hi! My name is Papa Joe. No, not really. My name is Joseph Herman Anthony Lubbehusen. That's quite a handle, isn't it?

I'm sure many of you have wondered how I got the name Papa Joe. So I have decided to satisfy everyone's curiosity. Nothing revolutionary or world shattering (or even interesting, perhaps) but it's how I got the name Papa Joe.

I was always called Joe or Joey as a kid, except when I did something bad or irritating to my mom and then it was "Joseph Herman Anthony!" When she called me by all three names I knew it was serious – I was in trouble and I should not have done whatever I did.

Yes, I was called a few other names when I spent three years in the Army during WWII. However, I don't think mentioning them now will help explain how I got the name Papa Joe. OK, so how did I get that moniker?

Here goes! When my wife and I started raising our family in Midland after our marriage, I took up bowling as a past time. The children all called me dad or father and no other name – that I'm aware of!

Sara Jane, our youngest child, came along five years after our third child so she was always kind of considered our baby (she'll kill me when she reads this!). When Sara became a teenager, for some reason or other, she decided to give her father a very special birthday present, a bowling shirt imprinted with PAPA JOE on the back. (One of my most favorite gifts ever received.)

I wore that shirt for many years and once almost rolled a 300 game. It was only a 278 but that's almost 300 isn't it? I also almost had a 700 series once. It was only a 686 series but it was close to 700! I do know for a fact that one year I did make the Midland City All Star team. Those were the years when bowling was bowling and not the easy stuff they call bowling today! Only kidding, all of you bowlers!

Even though a little tattered and worn, I still have that bowling shirt. Why? I'm waiting until I get a little older, don't have anything else to do and take up bowling again as a pastime. (And show those youngsters what bowling's all about. Again, I'm only kidding!)

So that wasn't such an earth shattering story, was it? I just wore that bowling shirt my sweet Sara gave me for my birthday for many years and now everyone calls me Papa Joe. Even my grandkids and they didn't even know I bowled!

I think the next time they come to visit I'm going to take them upstairs, show them my bowling shirt and tell them how I got my Papa Joe name. Yes, it's still up there in my closet because I just snuck up there and took a peek!

P.S. Did I ever tell you about my pet duck Goo Goo I had when I was a kid? Maybe the next time.

Humorous Banners – August 24, 2007

To the editor:

Hello to all my fellow 50-plus friends. I'm sure you are all interested in AARP activities, which help keep us informed about what is going on with our generation.

Well, good news! A very good friend of mine and a past president of AARP has just passed on to me some information which I think will be of interest to you. It is a promotional program they have going on utilizing banners. I would sure think the quotes on these banners are to, from and by senior citizens. See what you think.

I'm sorry I don't have the means to show you the banners but I can tell you what they say. I guess if you wanted more information you could contact AARP: OK, here goes, happy reading:

- Florida – God's waiting room.
- I must be getting older – all the names in my phone book end with M.D.
- I'm chronologically gifted – I am not old.
- Experience is a wonderful thing – It enables you to recognize a mistake when you make it again.
- Flowers – at my age, they scare me.
- I'm so old that when I eat out, they ask me for my money up front.
- I'm so old, all my friends in heaven will think I didn't make it.
- I believe in having sex on the first date – at my age, there may not be a second time.
- Birthdays are good for you – the more you have the longer you live.
- The only good thing about Alzheimer's – you get to meet new people every day.
- Support bingo – keep grandma off the streets.
- Retirement – twice as much husband, half as much money.

Well, there you are my good friends! Old Papa Joe would like to close with this piece of advice: "As you amble and ramble through life – whatever be your goal – keep your eye upon the donut, and not upon the hole." Peace!

Best Ever – October 27, 2007

To the editor:

Sincere thanks and appreciation go to all the kind and generous people who contributed to this year's successful Alzheimer's 2007 Memory Walk. Thank you for your contributions and thank you for walking. Extra special thanks to God for giving us such a beautiful short-sleeve sunny day.

I am happy to report my 15-year-old granddaughter Jamie Lynne was able to come and help us again for the third year. Not only did she bring her mother but her Uncle John, who flew in from Florida. My best walk ever!

The Mid-Michigan Walk not only includes Midland but Frankenmuth and Saginaw as well. Dawn Spicer, who was just promoted to regional director of the Mid0Michigan region (congratulations Dawn – great job!) has informed me that they have exceeded their goal for 2007 and are still counting.

Incidentally, just in case you forgot to mail in your contribution, it's not too late. Please send it to the Alzheimer's Association, 4604 N. Saginaw Road, Midland, MI 48640.

On behalf of my late wife, Marjorie Rose, who suffered from Alzheimer's, I am deeply appreciative of your support to help the Alzheimer's Association on their continuing work to find the cause and cure for this horrible disease. Thank you and may God always smile on you and keep you in the palm of his hand.

Here a Quote, There a Quote – November 8, 2007

To the editor:

One of the habits I have picked up over the years and still maintain is my "quote file." Every time I hear or see a memorable saying I put it in my quote file.

Recently, I must have been having a nightmare or something because for some reason this quote kept popping up in my dreams: "If you don't know what you're doing, don't do it!" Very profound, eh? I wonder what I was dreaming about?

Anyway, as I was putting this statement in my quote file I started looking at its contents and thoroughly enjoyed reading them. So, why not share some of them with my friends? Here you are – enjoy.

- Do something good for yourself – give someone a hug.
- The best way to stay young is to stay so busy you don't have time to grow old.
- A life filled with love will have some thorns, but only a life empty of love will have no roses.
- Smiling makes you happy! Or is it being happy makes you smile? Why don't we just do both and not be confused!
- I really do like who I am. And I really enjoy aging. If it didn't lead to death it would be perfect.
- Happiness is a perfume you cannot pour on others without getting a few drops on yourself.
- I try to learn from my mistakes – I'm pretty close to being a genius.
- Life may not be the party we hoped for, but while we're here, we might as well dance.
- Every time I hear the dirty word exercise – I wash my mouth out with chocolate.
- The key to happiness and a good enjoyable life is to have a good sense of humor.

There you are folks; just a few from my quote file. In closing, here's something else you might wish to consider as you ramble on through life. "Life's journey is not to arrive at your grave in a well preserved body, but rather to skid in sideways, totally worn out, shouting, "Wow, what a ride!" So keep a smile on your face, a song in your heart and don't sweat the little things in life – enjoy it!

Love Someone – February 6, 2008

To the editor:

I can't believe where all the time has gone. Jan. 29 was the one year anniversary since God took my sweet Marjorie Rose to join Him and His heavenly family.

Needless to say, I miss her terribly after 57 years of marriage. Even though she did not know me when I visited her, I could touch her, hold her hand, kiss her and know she was there and I could feel her presence. Now she's gone and I miss her and not being able to tell her: "I Love You."

No, I'm not going to give you a long dissertation on all the wonderful things about who my Margie was and what she did because if I did it would take up the entire newspaper. Suffice to say she was the most wonderful lady, wife, mother and grandmother in the world. Marge was a very dedicated registered nurse in her heyday and even went back to college at 49 to receive a fine arts degree, cum laude. Margie had some philosophical tendencies and once in a while would jot them down. Recently, I was going through some of her old notes and found the following message, handwritten with several scratched out changes on a tattered old piece of yellow dog paper. Here's what Marge had to say: "Reach out … and love one another."

Many people hide themselves behind a wall of illusion. They never glimpse the truth. Then it's far too late and they pass away. They talk about all the love we could share – when and if we find it.

With our love, we could save the world. All you have to do is realize it's all within yourself – no one else can make you change. But, the love has gone cold and people have also. People who gain the world and lose their soul – they don't know, they can't see. Are you one of them? And the time may come when we're all one. Where have all the people gone – is it too late to realize who our brother is?

I would like to add a postscript to Margie's note. It's all right to say "I love you" to someone everyday and obey our Lord's commandments in a real and vital way. The heart can be a lonely place when no one comes to call, but when someone says I" love you," it makes you feel 10 feet tall. Those three little words can mean so much and they're not hard to say, so it is all right to say "I love you" to someone every day. I love all of you!

Remembering a Remarkable Woman and Mother – May 11, 2008

As I was contemplating writing a commentary for Mother's Day, I got thinking about my own sweet departed mother. Not that I have ever forgotten her because I think of her and pray for her every day of my life. The more I think about her the more I realize how much of an amazing lady she was. Let me tell you a little bit about Philemena Oser Lubbehusen.

She was born in St. Henry, Ind., in 1882 and passed away in 1977 at the age of 95. The doctor said Mom died of old age. In those days when they couldn't properly identify the cause of death – it was due to "old age." I believe Mother just wore herself out.

Every time I think of my mom's maiden name, Oser, I can't resist wondering how uncomplicated my whole life might have been if my name had been Joe Oser. Not Joe who?, or how do you spell that?, etc. Just plain old Joe Oser. Wow!

I don't know anything about Mom's marriage, but when I was about 1-1/2 years of age, my father decided he no longer wanted to be married to my mother so he packed a suitcase and took off with another woman. My mother was left with the responsibility of raising and supporting seven children. I was the baby of the family.

As the cliché' goes, "we were as poor as church mice." We lived in a one-bedroom house (Mom's room) with no plumbing, heating, electricity and no telephone. All seven children slept in the unheated attic. The four girls, the oldest of the children, slept two to a bed and the three boys all slept in the same bed. I was the lucky one in the winter because I got to sleep in the middle.

The only way Mother knew how to support her seven children was to take in laundries and ironings. Mom did not have a washing machine or dryer but they wouldn't have helped much because, like I said earlier, we didn't have any electricity.

We hand-pumped water from our well and heated the water on our wood-burning stove. Mom washed and rinsed everything by hand and the clothes were hung outside on a clothes line tied from one tree to another, weather permitting. There were many days when the clothes had to hang inside the house, with the clothes line crisscrossing just about every area in the house. We did a lot of stooping when walking in the house on those days.

Mom was always the first one up in the morning and the last one to bed at night. Her first chores were to get the coal and wood stoves started for heat and to cook breakfast. "Eat your oatmeal, Joe, it will stick to your ribs and keep you warm!"

I don't think I ever heard my mother complain or tell us her problems. When I think back on her existence, it's hard to keep from crying – she had no one to hug her and kiss her and tell her how much she was loved and appreciated, except her seven young children.

Mom always served us hot breakfasts and suppers, nothing fancy or extravagant, but always hot, and we always ate together at the same time. We were just happy to have something to eat. We always said grace before a meal and gave thanks afterwards.

Mom was a small lady and I doubt if she weighed more than 110-120 pounds. I was always amazed by her strength and stamina. She must have fallen in bed every night completely exhausted. That happened after her kids were fed, did their homework and got ready for bed. But first, we all gathered and knelt around my mother's bed and said the rosary. Every night! That's what we did instead of watching TV – because there was no TV in those days. Unbelievable!

Every Saturday was "bath day." Mother would put a washtub of warm water behind the coal stove in the dining room and one by one all of us kids had a weekly bath – whether we needed it or not!

Christmas was always looked forward to with great anticipation because that was the only time we ever got anything. About a week or so before Christmas, Mom would close the door to the front living room and put newspaper over all the windows to keep us kids from peeping in. Naturally as Christmas got closer we would try to peep under the door but we could never get our faces close enough to the floor to see anything. Darn it!

On Christmas Eve, we always had oyster stew for supper. (Where did we get the oysters in Indiana?) After supper Mom would go into the front room, door still locked, and make a fire in the fireplace and light the candles on the Christmas tree. Yes, real candles!

When Mom had things ready, we were allowed to go (run) into the front room and get our presents. Normally it was clothing with one toy and a small sack of candy. After admiring our gifts and having some candy, it was time to put out the tree lights and go to bed, if you could sleep! Then around 11 p.m. we would get dressed and walk to Midnight Mass.

I guess things were quite different back in the 1920s and '30s, in that my mother never got a divorce or legal separation from her husband when he left her. Anyway, when he died many years later he was destitute, nearly blind, living in a boarding house with not a cent to his name. The owner of the house contacted my mother and told her that one of his last requests was to be buried back home with the rest of the family.

Mother, being the wonderful and outstanding lady that she was, took her very meager life savings, paid to have his body shipped back home and p aid all the expenses to bury him. But, not with the rest of the family – he had his own plot. My inheritance money (all $300) was spent to bury my father. Not my dad, because I didn't have one.

Well, I told you my mother was a fabulous person didn't I? Please do me a favor the next time you're saying your prayers and say one for Saint Philemena. I'm pretty sure that God has elevated her to that status for all the goodness she brought forth in her 95 years here on earth.

Golf Tips – May 28, 2008

To the editor:

Yep folks, I'm back from Florida and as reported earlier, we had a fantastic 11th annual snowbird blood drive and received donations of 428 pints of blood. My brief comment is WOW! My anti-terrorist beach duty was also very successful, with no enemies making it ashore while I was on duty. My fringe benefit was getting a nice tan – with no sunburn!

Needless to say I did not have time to play golf but I did pick up some hot golfing tips for all of my buddies back here in Midland. Enjoy.

- Golf can best be defined as an endless series of tragedies, observed by the occasional miracle, followed by a good bottle of beer.
- Golf: You hit down to make the ball go up. You swing left and make the ball go right. The lowest score wins. And on top of that, the winner buys the drinks!
- Golf is harder than baseball. In golf, you have to play your foul balls!
- The term "Mulligan" is really a contraction of the phrase "Maul-It-Again."
- A "gimme" can best be defined as an agreement between two golfers, neither of whom can putt very well.
- An interesting thing about golf is that no matter how badly you play, it is always possible to get worse.
- Golf is a hard game to figure out. One day you'll go out and slice it and shank it, hit into all the traps and miss every green. The next day you go out and for no reason at all you really stink.
- If your best shots are the practice swing and the "gimme putt," you might wish to reconsider this game.
- Golf is the only sport where the most feared opponent is You.
- Golf is like marriage: If you take yourself too seriously it won't work, and both are pretty expensive!
- The best wood in the bags of most amateurs is the pencil.

In conclusion, all Ii can say is "fore" and "keep your head down." And, as long as you have your head down you might want to say a quick prayer, such as, "Dear God, please help me hit the ball." But, if you don't, please don't sweat the little things, because you still have a few holes to play.

Letter from 16-Year-Old Granddaughter Helps Make Father's Day Brighter – June 15, 2008

To the editor:

It was easy for me to write a Father's Day letter this year because my young, beautiful and sweet 16-year-old granddaughter did it for me. I was going to say I don't know what prompted her to write it, but I guess her letter is self explanatory. Hope your readers enjoy it.

Dear Papa,

I was thinking about Father's Day and it made me think about all the reasons that I love you. Here are 10 of them to make you smile. There are a lot more than 10 but here are a few. They don't go in any order:

- I love you because you always make me smile.
- I love you because you care so much about me.
- I love you because you take care of grammie so good. (She was referring to my sweet, departed Marjorie Rose.)
- I love you because you are so good to me and Jakie Joe. (Her brother, my grandson.)
- I love you because you love life and everyone in it.
- I love you because you would give anybody the world if asked.
- I love you because you are fun to be around.
- I love you because you are so cool and hip. (Wow!)
- I love you because you are so nice to everybody.
- I love you because you love me!

Papa Joe, I am so glad that you got to come and see us. There are so many more reasons that I love you but I think it would take hours to write and it would probably take over 400 pages to do. I love you. Happy Father's Day.

Your Jamie girl,
Jamie S.

Needless to say I get very emotional reading and writing about Jamie's letter so I would just like to send her my quick reply. "Jamie I love you with my whole heart and soul and pray that God will always take good care of you. Love, Papa Joe."

P.S. Happy Father's Day to all of you wonderful "DADS" out there. You know who you are and so do all the loved ones to whom you give so freely of your love and time. God bless each and every one of you.

Cheers – July 23, 2008

To the editor:

Recently, a small group of my good friends – they are all good friends although the groups are getting smaller and smaller – were talking about the topic of drinking while we were sitting around philosophizing and enjoying a little libation – Iced tea and lemonade! We were discussing specifically how liquor affects the different species, including mankind.

The topic made me think of an article I had read many years ago so I got it out and read it to the group. I think your readers will also enjoy this little dissertation and facetious article entitled "Liquor Lengthens Life."

The horse and mule live 30 years
And know nothing of wine and beers.
Goats and sheep at 20 die
And never taste scotch or rye.
Cows drink water by the ton
At 18, they are mostly done.
The dog at 15 cashes in
Without the aid of rum or gin.
The cat in milk and water soaks
And then in 12 short years it croaks.

The modest sober, bone dry hen
Lays eggs for nogs, then dies at 10.
ALL ANIMALS are strictly dry.
They sinless live, and swiftly die.
But, sinful, ginful, beer-soaked men
Survive for three score years and 10!
And, some of them, a very few,
Stay pickled 'til they're 82.

Yes, there is a moral to this story – if ginful, sinful man can live to three score and ten, maybe if he quit drinking he might live to be four score and ten!

Oh yes, tis the summer season so I want to give you my yearly advice – don't drink and drive or you might end up as a dead duck, and they don't even drink. Dean Martin warns everyone also, "If you drink, don't drive. In fact, don't even putt!"

As I tell all my friends and share with you, too, may God watch over all of you and may you have a very long and healthy life.

Children Are the Best – August 8, 2008

To the editor:

Children! God bless each and every one of them – a dozen times! Two of my daughters and four grandchildren have been in town and I have thoroughly enjoyed them. They just left and journeyed up north to spend a week or two camping. Yes, I was invited to go but when I considered all the alternatives I decided I would be better off staying here at home and defending the fort. Besides, I had three years camping in Europe during World War II and I don't think I'm quite ready for any more for a while!

Now, back to the children. A good friend recently sent me some children stories that tickled my funny bone and I would feel remiss if I didn't pass them on to readers.

- A Sunday school teacher was telling her class the story of the good Samaritan. She asked the class, "If you saw a person lying along the roadside all wounded and bleeding, what would you do." A thoughtful little girl broke the hushed silence, "I think I'd throw up."
- A Sunday school teacher asked, "Johnny, do you think Noah did a lot of fishing when he was on the Ark?" "No," replied Johnny. "How could he, with just two worms."
- A rabbi said to a precocious 6-year-old boy, "So your mother says your prayers for you each night? That's very commendable. What does she say?" The little boy replied, "Thank God he's in bed!"
- During the minister's prayer one Sunday, there was a loud whistle from one of the back pews. Tommy's mother was horrified. She pinched him into silence and, after church, asked, "Tommy, whatever made you do such a thing?" Tommy answered soberly, "I asked God to teach me how to whistle, and he just did!"
- A Sunday school teacher said to her children, "We have been learning how powerful kings and queens were in Bible times. But, there is a higher power. Can anyone tell me what it is?" One child blurted out, "Aces!"

No offense to all you wonderful mothers out there, but this is my favorite of all the children stories.

Little Johnny and his family were having dinner at his grandmother's house. Everyone was seated around the table as the food was being served. When little Johnny received his plate, he started eating right away. "Johnny! Please wait until we say our prayer," said his mother. "I don't have to," the boy replied. "Of course you do," his mother insisted. "We say a prayer at our house before eating." "That's our house," Johnny explained, "but this is grandma's house and she knows how to cook."

Like I always say, "out of the mouths of babes." They rule the world so we don't really have to sweat the little things in our lives, do we?

"Bad Hair Day" a Reminder of Philosophy On Life – September 7, 2008

To the editor:

Papa Joe had a "bad hair day" recently. I honestly believe God gives them to me every so often so I will be reminded of one of my philosophies of life – "Don't' sweat the little things."

I had a meeting scheduled one afternoon but decided I still had time to run out to Meijers and do a little shopping. The shopping didn't take up much time but the visiting with all the friends I met was a little intensive. After some "goodbyes" and "see ya laters," I headed for home.

I put my groceries away and headed out for my meeting. As I passed the downstairs bathroom, I decided it might be a good idea if I used it before heading out. When I had finished, the toilet flushed and I was washing my hands, but something didn't sound quite right – the water was still running. I lifted the toilet seat just in time to see the water overflowing. I stood there in shock for a second or two trying to get my brain to function.

All I could think of was Towels! Towels! Towels! I ran out the back door to the garage – no towels in sight! I started for the upstairs when I remembered I had done a large load of towels that morning. I grabbed four large bath towels and headed back up the stairs.

By this time the bathroom floor was overflowing – water was pouring in the hallway on its way to the living room, basement steps and the kitchen floor. I put one towel down to block the flow to the basement, the next one to block the flow to the living room, and one to block the flow to the kitchen. The fourth towel went down right in the middle of the bathroom floor. When I got the water flow stopped, I started the process of picking up the towels and trying to get them to the sink to ring out the water.

I think most of you have experienced what I went through so I won't further describe my ordeal. Suffice to say, it was one big mess! I had to tell myself, "Chill out, Joe, and don't sweat the little things in life. Besides, now you have a clean bathroom, hallway and kitchen floor."

Ha! Ha! Ha!

But my bad hair day wasn't done. After everything was cleaned up, I decided I would make a pot of homemade chili. There's nothing better than a good bowl of homemade chili to perk a person up. When everything was ready, I took the pan of chili off the stove and turned around to place it on the counter. Guess what? Yep, a ladle of chili tipped over the side of the pan and all over my clean kitchen floor!

I immediately started to think of some "no-no" words when I again told myself, "Calm down, Joe, stay cool and remember, 'don't' sweat the little things in your life.'"

The chili ended up being fantastic, as was the glass of red wine I washed it down with. See folks, it's not too hard to stay cool and calm and not sweat the little things in life. But I didn't dare do the dishes and test my luck again. No three strikes and you're out for me! The dishes were still in the sink the next morning waiting for me. Amen!

Have a nice day everyone and keep smiling.

Hollywood Squares Answers Give us Something to Smile About – August 24, 2008

To the editor:

Ii have just come across some "oldage," which is a new word of mine meaning "old stuff from way back when." In past comments from some readers, most of them on the more mature side of life say they enjoy things from the good old days – back when we were young, carefree and happier than happy.

So, to all my good friends and everyone else who remembers the game show Original Hollywood Squares, here are some of the questions and answers, and responses that were spontaneous and clever and not scripted. I hope all your readers enjoy a day from the past.

Q. Do female frogs croak:

A. Paul Lynde: If you hold their little heads under water long enough.

Q. If you're going to make a parachute jump, at least how high should you be?

A. Charley Weaver: Three days of steady drinking should do it.

Q. According to Cosmo, if you meet a stranger at a party and you think that he is attractive, is it OK to come out and ask him if he's married?

A. Rose Marie: No, wait until morning.

Q. It is considered in bad taste to discuss two subjects at nudist camps. One is politics, what is the other?

A. Paul Lynde: Tape measures.

Q. Can boys join the Camp Fire Girls?

A. Marty Allen: Only after lights out.

Q. If you were pregnant for two years, what would you give birth to?

A. Paul Lynde: Whatever it is, it would never be afraid of the dark.

Q. According to Ann Landers, is there anything wrong with getting into the habit of kissing a lot of people?

A. It got me out of the army.

Q. While visiting China, your tour guide starts to shout, "Poo! Poo! Poo!" What does this mean?

A. George Gobel: Cattle Crossing

Q. Back in the old days when great-grandpa put horseradish on his head, what was he trying to do?

A. George Gobel: Get it in his mouth

Q. According to Ann Landers, what are two things you should never do in bed?

A. Paul Lynde: Point and laugh.

Well, what did you think? Subtle humor or what? The important question is, are you laughing? Now, don't sweat the little things, keep a smile on your face and the next time you see me, gimme a hug!

In the Palm of His Hand – October 11, 2008

To the editor:

This is a thank you letter to God. A little bit unusual, for sure, but I believe the circumstances warrant it.

I lost my dear sweet Marjorie Rose to Alzheimer's disease last year. Last December, the Love Light Trees had their 26th annual ceremony. I was invited but unable to attend. They were kind enough to send me an 8-inch battery-operated candle. The candles were lit during the program as a way to honor the lives they represent – in my case, my dear sweet Marjorie Rose.

I put the candle in the living room. Each evening when I adjourned to the living room I would turn on the light in memory of my wife and then turn it off when I retired for the night. Recently, when I went into the living room the light came on as I sat down. I guess Margie was a little anxious to see me that night and turned on the light herself. I had a wonderful time reminiscing with Margie that night!

A few weeks ago my youngest daughter came from Texas to visit. She suggested we cut some of my fresh dahlias and take them out to her mother's gravesite. A beautiful bouquet of flowers for a beautiful lady!

We sat on the bench in front of Margie's memorial and discussed what a wonderful woman she was. Then I took a walk so Sara could spend some special time alone with her mother. When I returned, Sara greeted me with a humongous smile and said, "Guess what, dad? There was just a beautiful hummingbird flying around Mom's grave."

No big deal, right? Maybe not to most people, but very significant to Sara and me. The hummingbird always was Margie's choice of God's many creatures. As I write this and look out the dining room window, I can see an 8x10 inch glass etched sculpture of two hummingbirds sipping on the nectar from the surrounding flowers – always one of Margie's favorites! As I walk around the corner to the bottom of the upstairs steps, I see on the wall a 27x21-inch copper patina etched hummingbird that Margie made herself, many years ago. Another reminder of the many wonderful years with Margie.

Now, why was that hummingbird flying around Margie's grave when Sara was visiting her mother for the first time since she died? Did Margie know Sara Jane had come all the way from Texas to visit her?

I guess the only thing I want to say is "God, mine is not to reason why, but wait until I die and then you can tell me why!" I also know I'm always safe with God holding me in the palm of his hand. Thank you God.

Don't Sweat It – December 1, 2008

To the editor:

It's been quite some time since I have sent any "ponderings" in for readers. I keep seeing them in my browser file and I'm getting to the point I'm wondering how, when and where myself! So, I'm going to send them to readers and let them ponder or whatever for a while. Here goes:

- Can you cry underwater?
- Why do they park in the driveway and drive in the parkway?
- How important does a person have to be before they are considered assassinated instead of murdered?
- Why do you have to "put your two cents in", but it's only a penny for your thoughts? Where's the extra penny going to?
- Once you're in heaven, do you get stuck wearing the clothes you were buried in for eternity?
- Why do doctors leave the room when you change? They're going to see you naked anyway?
- Why is "bra" singular and "panties" plural?
- If Jimmy cracks corn and no one cares, why is there a stupid song about it?
- If the professor on Gilligan's Island can make a radio out of a coconut, why can't he fix a hole in a boat?
- Why does Goofy stand erect while Pluto remains on all fours? They're both dogs!
- Why do the alphabet song and Twinkle, Twinkle, Twinkle Little Star have the same tune? (Why did you just try singing the two songs above?)
- Why do they call it an asteroid when it's outside the hemisphere, but call it a hemorrhoid when it's down below where the sun don't shine?
- Did you ever notice that when you blow in a dog's face, he gets mad at you, but when you take him for a car ride he sticks his head out the window?

(I think I figured that last one out – the dog is looking out the window to see if any of his friends are out there running around and playing without him!)

Now let me know how many you figured out. Not to worry though – don't sweat the small stuff, God's in charge! Go outside and take a walk, enjoy the nice weather, and thank God for all the good stuff He's done for you.

Stories Help Reveal the Meaning of Love – November 9, 2008

To the editor:

One of the greatest enjoyments of my life is when I'm out and about, any time of the day or night, and extend a "Good morning," or "Hi, how are you?" or some similar greeting to friends and especially, complete strangers. Then I look for the surprised look on the stranger's face. About 45 percent of the time, they will look at me with a smile on their face and reply, "Good, how are you?" Pretty nice, eh? Nothing like a warm fuzzy!

Everyone wants to be loved, or greeted with a "Hi, how are you?" But most of the time it has to be a friend first to get it back. Yes, it is a type of love I'm giving away and getting some of it back in return.

Love is a complicated subject for a lot of people, but I don't think it has to be. Love, I believe, is really simple. It's something I think about all the time, but sometimes it's pretty hard to explain or put into words. It is very simple, yet overwhelming. Confusing, eh?

Everyone has a soft spot in their heart, but for some reason or another, some people are reluctant to show or express it. What is love? Love comes in many sizes, shapes, and forms. Love can mean something different to each of us. I would like to pass on a story I read or someone passed on to me several years ago, which I interpret as one kind of love. See what you think.

An elderly gentleman had an early appointment with his doctor to remove some stitches from his hand. He told the nurse he was in a hurry as he had to get to the nursing home and help feed his wife breakfast. The nurse asked him if his wife would be worried if he was a little late.

The gentleman replied that his wife had Alzheimer's disease and she no longer knew who he was and had not recognized him in five years. The nurse was surprised to hear that and asked him, "Why are you still going to visit her every morning, even though she doesn't know who you are?" He smiled, patted the nurse's hand and said, "She doesn't know who I am, but I still know who she is!"

Now, is that love? I believe that true love can be neither physical nor romantic. True love is an acceptance of all that is, has been, will be, and will not be. That makes you stop and think for a minute, doesn't it?

I can personally relate to the above story with my sweet Marjorie Rose when she was still alive and in a nursing home. Friends often would ask me the same question, "Papa Joe, why do you always visit Margie three to four times daily when she doesn't even know you're there?" My reply was always the same, with a smile on my face. "She may not know who I am, but I still know who she is, and I was there because I loved her with my whole heart and soul!" Plus, I also snuck in a few kisses each visit!

I often have wondered if Margie knew I was visiting her, even in her earlier years of the disease. Only God knows and to what extent. I have a very fond memory of the last time I saw Marjorie Rose smile.

One of my daily morning routines after Marge had breakfast was to give her a Papa Joe "facial special," which consisted of a warm wash cloth facial, followed up with a lotion facial.

One day I was gently rubbing skin lotion on her face and neck, and on that particular day I inadvertently went a little lower than normal. I happened to glance up at Margie, who hadn't smiled for quite some time, but at the moment she had the biggest and happiest smile on her face that I had seen in months. That smile, that day, was worth more than thousands of daily visits, and I will never forget it until my dying day.

Did Margie know I was giving her a facial that day? Only God knows for sure, but I would bet a million dollars Margie knew it was old Papa Joe rubbing that lotion on her with a recognizable soft and gentle touch with lots and lots of familiar loving, tender care.

What Clothes Will We be Wearing in Heaven? – January 7, 2009

To the editor:

In one of my recent "ponderings" letters, one of the questions asked was: Once you're in heaven, do you get stuck wearing the clothes you were buried in for eternity? Good question, right? One that I bet you never thought about until now.

I seldom think about dying and I know it's inevitable at my age (don't ask!), but recently I did start thinking about that clothes deal.

In my final resting plans I have told the kids it was up to them as to whether or not they wanted an open or closed casket for my funeral. I told them that if it was an open casket, to make sure I had on one of my sporty outfits and if it was a closed casket, just a nice pair of shorts and one of my nice casual t-shirts.

Now, the more I think about the clothes I may have to wear for eternity, the more I started thinking I prefer the shorts and T-shirt. Why? I used to play a lot of golf in my younger days with a lot of my friends and good buddies, most of whom passed away in recent years. Needless to say, I have often wondered if we would ever meet again.

Then my mind jumped to dying and meeting St. Peter at the Golden Gates. After getting his approval and permission to enter – I hope! – I was going to ask him where the nearest golf course was. Also, would he please contact my old buddies Reggy, Smiley and Obbie and have them meet me there. Since this is heaven, we don't need a tee time do we?

Since we're in heaven I'm also sure they had Budweiser beer up here, so St. Peter, would you please have them put a six pack on each of our golf carts. I don't know if one gets thirsty or not in heaven but I just want to play it safe and be prepared by having the beer available.

Since we've in heaven I assume all my drives will be straight down the middle of the fairways and all my putts accurate. I don't care about my score just as long as I get a birdie once in a while.

Okay folks, are you dreaming along with me? Now you know why I want to be buried in my shorts and t-shirt. One question that I keep asking myself is, "I wonder what clothes my buddies were buried in?" Oh well, they never were very good golfers so they shouldn't have too much trouble playing golf in their suits – as long as there is plenty of Budweiser beer!

FORE! And keep your head down!

Walking and Talking – February 6, 2009

To the editor:

Several months ago, I was in the hospital for a routine test and one of the preps prior to the test was to sit quietly for an hour or so with a needle in my arm dripping some kind of a liquid in my arm. I think it was called hydration or hydrating or something like that. My personal preference for hydrating is not a needle in my arm, but a bottle in my mouth.

Anyway, I had plenty of time to think and for some reason or another (it was my 8? Birthday), I got to thinking about aging and how fortunate I was to still be alive and healthy. I attribute my situation to good genes (some of my family members made it to their 100s), positive thinking and lots of exercise, especially walking.

I firmly believe that exercise is the key to good health and aging. The more I thought about it, the more I thought that I had to share my wealth of knowledge with you couch potatoes out there. Maybe it will stimulate you to make your life more fulfilling! Seriously. Well, maybe a little facetiously. Listen up now!

- My grampa started walking five miles a day when he was 60. Now he's 96 but we don't know where he is.
- My brother Art is 86 (really!) and has been walking a golf course since he got out of the Marine Corps after WW2 in 1946. He's still trying to find a hole in one.
- Personally, I like to walk early in the morning before my brain figures out what I'm doing. One of the hardest things I'm having trouble with in my walking is to get over the hill.
- I know of a lady that doesn't walk and she has flabby thighs. Fortunately for her, though, her stomach covers them.
- I think an advantage of exercising every day is when I die, people will look at me and say, "Wow! He really looks good doesn't he?"
- I have had people often ask me if I'm getting fatter and I tell them, "No, but I am getting heavier as I age because there's more in my head." (That's my theory and I'm sticking with it!)
  AND
- Whenever I start thinking too much about how I look and feel, I just take a walk, find a Happy Hour somewhere, and by the time I leave I look fine – and I feel great too!

Now, whatcha going to do? I suggest you put a smile on your face, go take a walk in the mall and I'm sure you'll feel good about yourself. You may even run into some of your friends – walking I hope!

Peace!

Don't Sweat the Little Things, Even When Caught in a Downpour – March 30, 2009

To the editor:

Papa Joe has been home for a while now in good old Midland, Michigan. My tour of duty in Florida was relatively short this year due to a colder winter than normal, which does help prevent any terrorist activity. The only terror I experienced was thinking I was going to freeze one of those cold nights! I later found out what cold really was when I got back home. I'm not going to complain though as I know it has to get better here and I've put away my snow shovel and brought out my garden spade.

I do want to tell you about a little incident that happened to me this year. Like they say, "there's always a first time for everything." As your readers know, one of my anti-terrorist duties is patrolling the Naples Beach and making a 2.5-mile round trip to the pier once in the morning and again in the afternoon.

Normally everything is OK, but last year I did get a little scare. As I was walking toward the end of the pier I thought I saw some one-man submarines, but on closer examination, thank God, they were only a couple of large manatees. Oh, the price of patriotism! God bless America.

In all my years in walking back and forth to and from the pier, I have never been drenched in the rain like I was this year. I do mean drenched! On this particular day it was cloudy but nothing looked ominous or threatening.

Shortly into my walk, though, I started to feel a few rain drops. Luckily I saw a little Tiki Hut on the beach shore so I immediately headed for it. Thankfully, as it rained very hard for 10-15 minutes before letting up to a little drizzle.

What the heck I decided, it's only a little drizzle and I can beat it home before another down pour. WRONG!

I had only gone about a half block or so, when the gates of heaven opened. Since there was no place to go or hide, I proceeded to walk home in a steady downpour of rain and needless to say, got soaking wet. No big deal, it was chilly but not cold.

When I got near home, I decided to stop in at the neighbors and ask them if they had a dry towel I could use. Needless to say they just about died laughing when they saw this straggly old man standing there, soaking wet. They invited me in, offered me a dry towel and a glass of wine to warm me up. Not wanting to get their carpeting all wet and messy, I reluctantly declined their offer.

Instead I went directly home, had a nice warm shower, put on some dry clean clothes and had two glasses of wine to warm up, took a little nap while listening to some mellow Bob Marley reggae music.

It doesn't sound like much fun does it? Life can be very tough at times! But there is a moral in this story, the same as my lifestyle. "Take life a day at a time, with a positive attitude, smile, be happy and don't sweat the little things in your life – especially rain!"

A final comment from Mr. Wilson of Dennis the Menace fame who may dispute my philosophy as he recently remarked, "Whoever said 'Don't sweat the small things' never spent any time with Dennis the Menace." Amen.

Life Needs Laughter – April 15, 2009

To the editor:

Recently, while browsing through my book "A Letter of Love to My GRANDKids," I saw a short quote by Abe Lincoln that put a smile on my face. It was a quote that I was using in a dissertation to my grandchildren on the value of laughter.

I don't know who Abe was addressing in his talk, but it sounds like it was his Cabinet members. His quote was, "Gentlemen, why don't you laugh? With the fearful strain that is upon me day and night as president, if I did not laugh I should die. You need this medicine as much as I do!"

Quite a profound and philosophical statement by a very wise gentleman. Life is full of assaults on the human will. Yet, in the face of severe adversity, funny things happen from time to time and it does us a lot of good to laugh.

In the same letter to my grandkids, I mentioned an article by a former editor of the Saturday Review. He described his experience with a painful and debilitating illness. He wrote, "10 minutes of genuine belly laughter had an anesthetic effect and would give me two hours of pain-free sleep!" (Laughter is a pretty powerful medicine, isn't it?)

I think we all have learned that hearty laughter is a natural antidote to stress. We just have to learn to laugh more frequently. I was telling the grandkids that laughter increases the heart rate, blood circulation and blood oxygen levels, expands the lungs, raises the body temperature and lowers blood pressure.

I specifically pointed out to the ladies (my three youngest granddaughters) that laughter releases muscular skeletal tension and to "laugh as frequently as possible as it will help make you more beautiful!" Needless to say that was good for several smiles from the ladies.

Victor Borge once said, "Laughter is the shortest distance between two people." Why don't we compromise Vic? How about "hugging and laughing" is the shortest distance between two people?

Life is bittersweet – adversity abounds and laughter prevails. We don't laugh because we're happy, we're happy because we laugh. My final admonition to the grandchildren in my article was to always smile, but better yet, laugh, laugh, laugh! And remember, "Laugh and the world laughs with you – snore, and you sleep alone!"

Getting Curious – May 21, 2009

To the editor:

One of my key philosophies has always been to take life one day at a time because there ain't no tomorrow! But that has not stopped me from occasionally wondering what the future had in store for me "tomorrow."

I have always said, half kiddingly but more seriously now that I'm getting closer to my goal, that I am going to live to be 100. That is, until recently when I was having some standard "old age" tests and the doctor asked me if I took naps in the afternoon. When I told him occasionally he said, "Joe, if you take a one hour nap every day you will live another five years longer." "Wow, what a deal," I thought to myself.

So, let's see now, if my math is correct and I take that nap every day, plus my 100 years, I'm going to live to be 105 or live until the year 2029. Now I'm starting to get a little more curious and I'm starting to wonder what things will be like in another 20 years – "tomorrow." The first thing I tried to do was to review in my own mind what's going on today and then what possible direction can it go tomorrow. Wow! Mind-boggling!

So, after some lengthy consideration, prognostication and extrapolation, I have certainly ascertained that in the year 2029 we will be reading the following or very similar headlines. Good luck!

"Ozone created by electric cars now killing millions in the seventh largest country in the world, Mexifornia, formerly known as California."

"Baby conceived naturally! Scientists stumped."

"Couple petitions court to reinstate heterosexual marriages."

"Castro finally dies at age 112: Cuban cigars can now be imported legally, but President Chelsea Clinton has banned all smoking."

"George Z. Bush says he will run for president in 2036."

"Postal service raises price of first class stamp to $17.89 and reduces mail delivery to Wednesdays only."

"85-year, $75.8 billion study: Diet and exercise keys to weight loss."

"Average weight of Americans drops to 250 pounds."

"Global cooling blamed for citrus crop failure for third consecutive year in Mexifornia and Floruba."

"Abortion clinics now available in every high school in United States."

Well, are you ready for your opinion? Normally I give a conclusion to my letters to the editor, but I'm going to forego one today. I suggest readers have that honor. Whatcha think folks?

"Click It or Ticket" Campaign Reminder of Tragic Accident Years Ago – June 7, 2009

To the editor:

During the past week or so I have been hearing some spot commercials by The United States Department of Transportation which were entitled "Click It or Ticket." I think the statement is self explanatory. It reminded me of one I had heard in the past and wrote a letter about it to the editor back in 2002. Please, let me repeat some of that story for the edification of some readers who may not have seen it but also as a reminder to everyone who drives.

Back in the year 1977, two of my lovely daughters were home visiting us over a long Memorial Day weekend. Since the girls hadn't seen each other for quite some time, they decided to go shopping. When they weren't home for dinner, we started worrying. Then the telephone started ringing and it was the police department informing us that our daughters had been in a very bad accident. Unfortunately one of the girls, who had only been married a couple of weeks, was killed instantly.

They were on their way home from shopping and only a few blocks away when a car swerved, hit the curb and rolled over. How could this terrible result happen when they were only driving 25-30 miles an hour down a three lane one way street? Why? Because the girls, after they had stopped at a nearby store for some evening snacks, forgot to put on their seat belts.

I don't think I have to go into any more details but I think you can understand why I'm writing this letter in support and endorsement of the "Click it or Ticket" campaign.

Please dear friends, it only takes a few seconds to "buckle up." I'm sure you'll feel safer and more secure and it could save your life or one of your loved one's life. I have a slogan I would like to give you: "Click It and don't take a chance of getting a Ticket – to St. Peter and the Golden gate."

The Apron – June 23, 2000

To the editor:

The other day I received an article from an old friend that brought many smiles to my face. I don't know who actually wrote this dissertation, but whoever did had to have lived through those wonderful experiences. Let me tell you about this story. Your current age will determine the amount of your smiles.

In the past I have written a couple of articles about my dear departed mother, Philomena (Minnie), and how she raised seven children by herself. Mom supported us by taking in washings and ironings. None of the kids were old enough to work so mom had to do everything by herself, which was a horrendous thing to do back in the 1920 and 1930 depression years.

Mom washed everything on a hand scrub board because she did not have a washing machine or dryer. As I have mentioned in the past, it wouldn't have done her any good because we didn't have indoor plumbing or electricity, etc., etc.

I think that gives you an idea of the trials and tribulations our parents and grandparents had back years ago. Now I want to tell you about "The Apron."

The principle use of the apron in those days was to protect the dress underneath as she only had a couple and it was easier to wash aprons than dresses and they used less material. Along with that, the apron was wonderful for drying children's tears, and on occasions was used for cleaning out dirty ears. From the chicken coop, the apron was used for carrying eggs, fussy chicks and sometimes half-hatched eggs to be finished in the warming oven.

When company came, those aprons were ideal hiding places for shy kids. When the weather was cold, grandma wrapped it around her arms. Those big aprons wiped many a perspiring brow, bent over the hot wood stove.

Chips and kindling wood were brought into the kitchen in that apron. From the garden, it carried all kinds of vegetables. After the peas had been shelled, it carried out the hulls. In the fall it was used to bring in apples that had fallen from the trees.

When unexpected company came up the road to visit, it was surprising how much furniture that old apron could dust in a matter of seconds.

Well, how many of you now remember the good old days? It will be a long time before someone finds something that will replace the apron, which served so many purposes. The last couple of generations probably don't have any idea about what was just written to why don't some of you grandmas and grandpas sit down with the grandkids and tell them the story of grandma's apron. It will be a good history lesson for those who have no idea of how important a part the apron played in our lives.

One final remembrance: Grandma used to place her hot baked apple pies on the windowsill to cool. Now granddaughters place theirs on the windowsill to thaw. They would go crazy now trying to figure out how many germs were on that apron. All seven of us kids lived into our eighties and nineties and I don't remember any of us ever catching anything from that apron – except love.

The Clothesline – July 13, 2009

To the editor:

As I was writing about the apron, my mind kept drifting to the clothesline, which also brought back many fond memories of the past. It was not only a very important part of life, like the apron, it was part of our everyday life – the entire neighborhood.

The clothesline was the neighborhood news bulletin and there were no secrets to be hid. Everyone knew if company would stop by the neighbors for a day or two. If so, you'd see the fancy sheets and towels on the line as well as the "company table cloth" with the fancy intricate design.

The clothesline announced a baby's birth by the new infant's clothes. You could also tell how much children had grown by how much the sizes of their clothes changed. It was easy to tell when sickness struck, as extra sheets, night clothes and maybe a bathrobe were hung on the line.

Gone on vacation was easy to tell as the clothesline was bare. You also could tell when people were back home because the line was no longer limp and sagging.

Clotheslines now are more or less a thing of the past because electric dryers do all the work. And, now whatever goes on inside a neighbor's house is anybody's guess! Gone are those good old days of the past when we knew a lot about our neighbors by what hung on the clothesline.

No, my story has not come to an end yet, not until I tell you an adventurous story about the clothesline and Papa Joe. My interest always was stimulated when I saw that sagging clothesline, tied up by each end to a couple of trees or a shed or whatever, and held up somewhat taut by a long wooden pole.

Where did I ever get the idea that I could take that wooden pole and use it to vault over that clothesline? But I did! Why not? What would be so hard about that? Positive thinking – I knew I could do it!

So one day I took that pole in both hands with a vaulter's grip and made a running approach toward the clothesline. At the proper distance (what's that?) I jabbed the pole into the ground and just as I was starting to make an elevated approach toward the line, I heard a snap and the next thing I knew I was in descent instead of ascent. The wooden pole had broken.

As I was descending, I quickly put my arms down to break my fall which was quickly followed by a snap or crack and this time it was my left wrist instead of the pole. Now that's the end of my clothesline story. Wasn't it exciting?

I guess I could tell you about my streetcar ride to the hospital for a "wrist job" but that wasn't all that exciting either. I do know that I gave up pole vaulting after that day and took up ping pong. It's not exciting but a lot safer.

A Step Back in Time: Remembering Goo Goo, the Pet Duck – August 23, 2009

Most children have a pet when they're young, mostly a puppy or kitten. However, no Lubbehusen kids had a pet. I guess Mom was busy enough and had enough trouble taking care of and feeding us kids. However, Lil Joe, the baby of the family, was a fortunate victim of circumstances and I did have a pet, a pet duck. Let me tell you how it all came about.

It seems that since I was the youngest child and around the house, whenever Mom wanted something from the corner grocery store, I was the gofer. One day Mother sent me to the store for a dozen eggs. They didn't come in one dozen cartons in those days but stored in large bins like they display fruits and veggies today.

If you wanted a dozen eggs, you took a small paper sack and filled the sack with the amount of eggs you wanted. As I was picking out eggs that day I noticed that one was larger than the other ones and also had a greenish color to it. Being inquisitive, I asked the grocer what it was and he told me it was a duck egg. Needless to say, I had to have that egg, so I put it in my sack to take home.

I jubilantly walked home with my new discovery, anxious to tell someone about my duck egg. It turned out to be, fortunately for me, my oldest brother, Buddy. As is to happened, Buddy had a few chickens that he was raising at the time and one of the hens was getting ready to set. (A little side note: Anyone could raise chickens in the city in those days, but now it's against the law. Silly, eh? As Mom would say, "This world is going to hell in a hand basket!)

Buddy suggested we put the duck egg with the chicken eggs the hen was setting on. "Will it hatch?" I asked. Buddy said he didn't know, but what did we have to lose – except my duck egg!

I can't remember exactly how long it was, but several weeks later Buddy called me down to the barn to show me something. "Guess what? The mother hen was walking around followed by several little chicks and a very cute little yellow duckling." What a sight! All those little chicks following their mother and this one little duckling waddling along, trying to keep up with them. A sight that I will remember the rest of my life.

The chicks and little duckling were all pecking and scratching around in the dirt and for some reason or other

I thought they needed some water. I got one of mom's pie tins from the kitchen and pumped some well water and set it down on the ground for my new friends.

The little chicks eventually walked up to the pie tin and stuck their beaks in the water and took a sip or two. Not my duckling though, who proceeded to crawl right into the pan of water and splash around. That was the first thing I learned about ducks – they need a larger pan of water than baby chicks. No, make that a larger pan of their own water!

For the life of me, I can't remember where or how I came up with the name, but from that point on my duck was called Goo Goo.

The mother hen more or less adopted Goo Goo and vice versa. Every place the hen and chicks went, my duck was sure to follow. However, as they matured and started going their own ways, my little friend would follow me around when I was in the backyard.

Incidentally, I didn't know what Goo Goo's gender was and never ever gave it a thought. Then one day I learned that Goo Goo was a she! How did I learn that? She laid on egg! From that day forward, I had a duck egg just about every morning for breakfast.

The first trick I taught Goo Goo was to play catch. I would take small pieces of bread and toss them into the air and she would catch them in her beak and amazingly she never missed. Normally when I played catch with her it was near her water pan because she liked to dunk her bread in the water.

Another memorable sight was when I was digging up Mom's garden getting it ready to plant her veggies. Goo Goo loved to eat earthworms! So when I was digging up the dirt, Goo Goo would get right in the middle of the garden with me and as I turned over the soil she would snatch and eat as many earthworms as she could find.

Unfortunately, one day Goo Goo got a little too anxious and got too close to my spade. One of the spade prongs pierced her webbed foot. It didn't seem to affect her, though, as she didn't cry out in pain or anything. I guess there were no nerve endings or feelings so I just kept on digging and Goo Goo kept one eating!

One of the first things I learned about ducks is that they poop a lot. I mean a lot! So you can understand the problem I had when I took Goo Goo to the fire station. The firemen wouldn't clean up after her so they made me do it. Since I didn't like cleaning up duck poop, I quit taking Goo Goo to the fire station.

Whatever happened to Goo Goo? When I eventually graduated from the eighth grade I went to a seminary to study for the priesthood. (Yep, it could have been Father Joe instead of Papa Joe!)

Shortly after I got to school, I got a letter from mom telling me that Goo Goo was missing and they didn't know what had happened. They speculated that someone walking down the alley behind our barn took her. We never did find out what happened to her.

Now, I couldn't end this story without a happy ending. When I was in the sixth grade ready to graduate into the seventh and eighth grades, it was also time for our individual yearly graduation picture. My teacher at the time was Sister Claudia and one of the strictest teachers I ever had.

However, Sister Claudia was aware of my pet duck situation and told me I could have my graduation picture taken with Goo Goo. What a thrill! So, my happy ending to this story is to show you my graduation picture taken with my pet duck, Goo Goo. What a handsome couple, eh?

Birthday Serves as Reminder of Philosophy of Life – October 19. 2009

To the editor:

Happy birthday to me! Happy birthday to me! Now, if I only had a big German chocolate cake with 85 candles to light. The only problem would be, who is going to help me below them all out? Maybe we could use a string of Christmas tree lights and just pull out the plug.

Often when people learn how old I am, they say, "Boy, you really don't look that old!" We all know that looks can be deceiving. But one thing I have learned in life is to never interrupt someone when you are being flattered! I thank them for their nice comment but I still know that I am 85, regardless of my looks!

I am taken back sometimes by that old man in my mirror. I am blessed to have lived long enough to have my hair turn gray. Or is it silver? Yes, there is a bald spot on the back of my head but that doesn't bother me because I can't see it. And those etched grooves in my face are due to my frequent and youthful laughter. Ha! Unfortunately, too many people have never really laughed and some have even died before their hair could turn gray or they could develop wrinkles.

You can tell the age of a tree by counting the rings in the trunk. I think you can tell the age of some people by counting the fun things they have stopped doing. So, come on folks, start doing those fun things again and get some gray hair and wrinkles!

Okay, now comes the moment of truth and the reason am writing this article. I have learned something that could prolong your longevity. I have lived 85 years and I've got another 20 years to go. How do I know that and why do I say that? Let me explain. I recently had my annual physical and while going through the stress tests, the doctor asked me if I took daily naps. I replied, "No, just once in awhile."

He then proceeded to tell me that if I took an hour nap every day, I would live another five years. Wow! I told him I was going to start immediately taking a daily hour nap and live to be 105. I explained this to him by telling him I was already planning to live to 100 because of my family genes and the extra five from napping would make it 105. Whatcha think? Does the doctor know what he's talking about? Regardless of the final results, I am still enjoying the nice naps!

Now I'm going to offer some philosophies of life that I try to live by. I believe in being yourself and doing what comes naturally. Be yourself and do whatever you want to whenever you want to. Don't worry about what people will think. You're not hurting anyone by being yourself and expressing your feelings.

I truly believe that the more you express yourself and your feelings, the happier you'll be – and that's what life is all about, being happy. It's contagious, just like a smiling face. If you smile at someone they will generally smile back at you and then you have two happy people. Now all we have to do is get half the people to smile and we'll have the whole world smiling. Remember what they say, "Smile and the world smiles with you; laugh and the world laughs with you; snore and you sleep alone."

One of the things I have learned in my journey through octogenarianship (that's a new word of mine) is that the healthiest seniors I know refuse to act their age. I also believe the key to their happiness is a positive attitude. When you think positive, your whole life will be positive. I firmly believe that a positive attitude, a good sense of humor and the ability to live one day at a time, not sweating the little things in life, will definitely help us all maintain a long, healthy and happy life.

To put it more succinctly: "Life's journey is not to arrive at your grave safely in a well preserved body, but rather skid or slide in sideways – totally pooped out – shouting "Wow, what a great ride I had in life." Thank you, God!

No Reason to Worry – February 13, 2010

One of the biggest frustrations in my life is the inability to really express how I feel about certain things. I have come to the conclusion we can best feel and express it if we take life one day at a time. Don't worry about the little things, have a good sense of humor with a positive attitude and a smile on your face.

My philosophy boils down to this: "Yesterday is history, tomorrow is a mystery, but today is the present; a gift from God!" Live each day to the fullest! Laugh heartily, love deeply, pray daily and let the rest of the world roll along as it comes. Surround yourself with positive people and positive things.

Sure, we all have bad days, but try to forget them as quickly as possible, and one way to do that is thank God for all the good days in your life.

A lot of people spend too much time working on long-term goals to a better life, and tend to forget that day to day things are what our lives are all about, and that includes the ups and downs. We can't let our lives slip through our fingers by thinking about the past, nor about the future – the present is what our lives are all about.

I don't believe there is much happiness in life until we learn to relax and really enjoy the process of living. Do not run through life so fast that you forget where you are and also where you're going. Life is not a race, but a journey to be savored each step of the way. So, slow down! Take the time to smell the roses – it could be later than you think!

I am now at a junction in my life where I have never been happier – even though I am an octogenarian. (Boy, that word used to scare the heck out of me, but now I consider anyone under 90 young.)

Yes, I've had a lot of trials and tribulations in my life and I am now experiencing senior citizen trials and tribulations but I still enjoy people and everything in my life more than I ever have. Sound a little weird? Not when you realize these good feelings are the result of a good sense of humor and a positive attitude. I try to find humor in everything, and not to take myself too seriously. I can and do laugh at my "goofs" in life.

I believe that a positive attitude means happiness and it is a well-known medical fact that happy people have fewer health problems and live longer. If you're happy, you laugh more and if you laugh more, you smile more. Who can deny a smile? Smiling makes you laugh – or is it laughing makes you smile? Let's do both and the whole world will be happy and smiling.

Worry is another problem in some people's lives. I have learned that I cannot do anything about those bad things that have happened to me, so why worry about them? I read that about 95 percent of the things people worry about involve something they think is going to happen, but doesn't happen. So why worry? Why not celebrate and only worry about the 5 percent? Why even do that? The 5 percent are little things and we don't sweat the little things, do we?

In my "Papa Joe" book I started writing back in 1993 I have a story about worry. I don't know where I got it, but I'm not going to worry about it. Here it is.

WORRY

There are only two things to worry about in your life – either you get sick or you are well. If you are well, there is nothing to worry about, but if you are sick, then there are still only two things to worry about – whether you will get well or die. If you get well, then there is nothing to worry about, but if you die, you still have two things to worry about –whether you will go to heaven or hell. If you go to heaven, then there is nothing to worry about, and if you go to hell, there is nothing to worry about either because you will be so busy shaking hands with all your friends that you won't have time to worry.

So, stop worrying – there's nothing to worry about!

Hand Gestures – February 25, 2010

To the editor:

Recently I heard a story about a foreigner who was driving on the Detroit freeway when another car passed him and gave him a hand gesture. Not knowing American customs and since it was the holiday season, the foreigner thought the gesture meant happy holidays.

While we all know the gesture meant something entirely different, it reminded me of a story. Several weeks ago I was in a religious book store when I saw a bumper sticker that read, "HONK IF YOU LOVE JESUS."

I am certainly glad that I purchased that sticker because of the uplifting experiences that followed.

One day, I was stopped at the light at the Eastman/Saginaw intersection, lost in thought. I didn't notice right away that the light had changed.

Boy, I learned very quickly that the bumper sticker worked. I found out that a lot of people love Jesus! The guy in the car behind me started honking and then the cars behind him started honking.

Somewhat elated, I waved and smiled at all those loving people. I think one of them was from Florida because I could hear him yelling something that sounded like "sunny beach."

Several other drivers got caught up in the joy of the moment and started honking their horns and they all started giving me what my grand kids called the Hawaiian Good Luck Sign. About that time, I stepped on the gas and got the heck out of there. Probably a good thing, because I was the only car to get across the intersection.

As I drove off, I looked back at all those drivers sitting there and I gave them all a big smile and the Hawaiian Good Luck Sign in return. Boy, I sure thank and praise the good Lord for such a large group of people who love Jesus.

Well, dear Pilgrims, whatcha think? That's my story and experience with my new bumper sticker. Personally I prefer a two finger salute which means "peace" to the single finger Hawaiian Good Luck Sign. Even better yet, if any of us feel inclined to any kind of hand gesturing, I think it should be to fold our hands in front of us, bow our heads and thank God for all the good and wonderful things he has bestowed upon us and how very fortunate we are just to be alive.

Thoughts About St. Patrick's Day – March 16, 2010

To the editor:

I generally write a St. Patrick's Day letter just because it's St. Patrick's Day, but this year I have an ulterior motive that I'll explain later on.

I believe I got more involved in St. Patrick's Day after I retired and started wintering in Naples, Florida. The city of Naples has a humongous parade every year. It got bigger each year – bag pipers and kilties galore!

After the parade my snowbird friends, Margie and I would all go out and celebrate with the Irishmen and the "Irishmen for the day." Our gang would hit a few pubs for some green beer and eventually a nice restaurant for some corned beef and cabbage.

Since this is a St. Patrick's Day letter, I probably should give you some facts and fables about our guest of honor. Many of you will probably be surprised to learn that St. Pat was not Irish. He was a Roman and his name was Patricius Magonus Sucatus.

When Patricius was 16, the district in which he lived was raided by pirates and he spent the next six years working as a swineherd (one who tends swine) and praying for freedom and an escape.

During his captivity he developed a love for Ireland and its people. He went on to be a priest, then a bishop, and returned to do missionary work there. He is credited with converting the Irish paganism to Christianity, which is probably one of the things that led him to his sainthood.

One of the things St. Pat was not successful at was convincing the Irish the benefits of abstinence from drinking. He was credited, though, with getting rid of all the snakes in Ireland.

We have all heard the old rumor that there never were any snakes in Ireland, only that the Irish drank so much, they thought they were seeing snakes. Just a rumor!

I also once heard a story that when St. Pat was trying to get rid of the snakes he had a problem with a particular venomous snake that refused to leave. So St. Pat invited him into a special snake-ridding box he had made.

When the snake refused, saying the box was too small, St. Patrick asked the snake to prove it by slithering inside. When the wicked snake answered the challenge, St. Pat shut the box and threw the snake into the sea. St. Pat showed a lot of imagination and cunning, didn't he?

Now for the big question, "Why did I decide to write this St. Patrick's Day letter?" Well, I got to thinking about all the good times in Naples when I would get together with all my snowbird friends and celebrate by going out for a corned beef and cabbage dinner and washing it down with green beer. Now my good friends, my question for you is "Where can I go in, or near, Midland to get a good corned beef/cabbage dinner with some non-alcoholic green beer on St. Patrick's Day?" Like I said before, on St. Patrick's Day, everyone, even a good German like myself, is a little Irish. My phone number is (989) 631-6034.

Yes, March 17 is St. Patrick's Day, but more important to me is March 19, which is St. Joseph's Day, my patron saint's namesake day. Yes, I will celebrate St. Joseph's Day in my own way, as I kneel by the side of my bed that night and thank St. Joe for being such a wonderful husband of Mary, the mother of Jesus. Yes, I'll even say a few "thank you" prayers to Jesus for all of the wonderful things he has done for me and given me for the past 85 years. And yes, I'll even offer him my thanks and appreciation for the corned beef and cabbage. I hope to enjoy on St. Patrick's Day. Erin Go Bragh!

Dwell on the Good Things – March 31, 2010

To the editor:

Quite some time ago, I started writing a story about a lady I had met earlier but for some reason I got distracted and never wrote it. I do remember it was something about her always complaining, and me giving her a dissertation on positive thinking. So here's the story.

One day as we were talking she asked me why I was always so happy. Briefly I told her God had been very good to me all my life and those positive things made me happy and helped give me a good sense of humor. I told her she should adopt the same attitude and be thankful for the good things in her life and not dwell on the negatives. Think positive!

I don't think my pep talk had helped her yet and she didn't have much to say about her life except she was always tired. I suggested she go to a doctor and get some medicine to help her out. She had no serious health problems – she was just getting old. She needed cheering up as we all do from time to time.

She was quite surprised when she inquired about my health and I told her I had two types of cancer. She wondered how I could always be so happy and upbeat. I told her God was in charge and since there wasn't anything I could do, except what the doctors told me to, why worry? I was still happy for all the good things in my life and I was just happy to be alive.

She said goodbye, turned around and went about her errands without another comment. I hoped that the next time I saw her she would have a more positive attitude. Sure enough, she did have a smile on her face the next time I saw her!

Maybe my message got to her!

Not much of a story, I know, but I just wanted to share my positive approach to life with you and hopefully put a smile on your face, make you happy and remind you to live and enjoy your life one day at a time and always with a positive attitude. And, don't sweat the little thing in your life.

Peace and good will to you all.

Odds and Ends – April 9, 2010

To the editor:

Back in the good old days (the early '70s) when I was still working at Dow Corning Corp., one of my responsibilities was to write a monthly report for the department. It didn't take me too long after I started to realize that my reports were a bunch of facts and figures – boring numbers with very little humanity.

So I started including some "highlights" of the department's personnel – promotions, transfers, marriages, new baby additions, etc. – just about anything or any activity that might be of interest to my report recipients.

Needless to say, old Papa Joe had to include his two cents worth of humor, so I started adding some "odds and ends" to cheer up the troops. Guess what? I recently found some portions of those old reports! I got a smile on my face reading some of my old highlights and decided to send a few your way. Hope you enjoy them.

ODDS AND ENDS – 1-20-75

- Bart claims he visited a zoo and saw a white rhinoceros being fed champagne – just think, an albino rhino wino.
- Don't know if this is true or not, but someone said they asked an employee if he wanted white wine or red wine and he said, "Doesn't make any difference to me, I'm color-blind."
- John says he only worries about two things – that conditions may never get back to normal, and that they already have.
- We, the willing, led by the unknowing, are doing the impossible for the ungrateful. We have done so much, for so long, with so little, that we are now qualified to do anything for nothing.

Something to be Said About Sharing a Smile with Others – June 2, 2010

As most of your readers know, I am a happy, smiley kind of guy and I would like to impart some thoughts about smiling in relation to a couple of recent events in my life.

I went to the mall recently to take my daily walk and on my journey around the mall I noticed a cute little blond girl, maybe 3-4 years old, dancing around in circles all by herself. Her grandma and grandpa were sitting nearby on a bench watching her frivolity with a smile on their faces.

Being in a frivolous mood myself, I started dancing as the little girl was doing. After awhile, I asked her if she could spin around as she danced. She tried to, but stumbled, as I did when I also tried the move. Both of us laughed at each other's clumsiness.

As the little girl and I continued our dancing, laughing and enjoying each other, her grandma and grandpa laughed and applauded us. It wasn't more than a minute or two before I noticed that a crowd of people had stopped by and were enjoying our show. All were laughing and applauding this little 3-4-year-old child and an 80+ old gray haired man having the time of their lives. Conclusion: age is no barrier to happiness, laughing and enjoying life. Try it, you might like it!

I recently went to the credit union to withdraw some money to send to the grandkids. When I approached the receptionist's desk, she asked me if I wanted to see one of the administrative assistants (or whatever they're called) and she asked me my name so she could sign me in. I replied Joseph Herman Anthony Lubbehusen. She then asked me how I spelled it and I replied J-O-E. "No, no," she said, "I already have Joseph written down, how do you spell your last name?"

Being in a frivolous mood, I very slowly spelled L-U-B-B-E-H-U-S-E-N-S-K-I. About that time, she looked up at me laughing and said "Why don't I just tell her Joe is here to see her?" Then we smiled at each other and had a good laugh.

See how much pleasure you can get out of life just by smiling and laughing? A good sense of humor is good for you! Bob Hope put it into perspective when he joked, "Have you ever heard of a laughing hyena with a heart burn?" Laugh and the world laughs with you – sing and everyone disappears!

Happiness is a smile. I have no trouble getting mothers with little babies to smile. I just ooh and aah and tell the mother how beautiful her baby is and she will "smile a mile!"

Then there are the grumpy, unhappy little kids who are out grocery shopping with mom instead of being at home playing with their friends. Mom is no bundle of joy, either, putting up with her unhappy kid. So, what I do is approach the mother holding up a Tootsie Roll, out of sight of the child and I quietly ask her if it's OK to give it to her child? If she nods her head or says, "Yes," I approach the child and say, "Hi, my name is Papa Joe. Would you like a Tootsie Roll?"

There is an immediate smile on the child's face as he reaches out for the candy, but I tell him he can't have it without asking his mother. If mom says OK, I give the child the candy. Then, as I walk away to do my shopping, both mother and child are smiling and happy. See how easy it is to get a smile out of two grumpy people with only one small Tootsie Roll?

A smile doesn't cost much, but sure gives a lot. When we smile, the world smiles back at us. Just try it the next time when you go shopping. Smile at the cashier or clerk and watch the pleasant attitude on their part. When we smile at someone, it makes them feel warm and welcome. I think I have a solution to the dilemma some people have with smiling. When you go into the bathroom each morning, look into the mirror and repeat this several times while smiling at yourself: "I am a very nice person and I like myself." Keep smiling as you brush your teeth. You will brighten your teeth and your smile, all at the same time. It really works – try it!

As I write this, I am also promising myself to smile a whole lot more. I once read where Dear Abby said it only takes 13 muscles to smile. I don't know what the heck that means, but I do resolve to smile more often. May God bless you all.

Proofreading Needed – August 8, 2010

To the editor:

I don't normally write about politics or religion. The last time, and maybe the only time, I wrote about religion I was criticized. I made the suggestion that I thought it was better to go to church on Sunday instead of playing golf. I won't go into what a reader had to say about my article, but I still think I'm right!

Anyway, this is not about religion per se, so I think I'm OK. This is about something my dear sweet daughter, Sally, school teacher, mother and sometimes proofreader of my letters, sent me.

Sally sent me some statements that were taken from several church bulletins or magazines. Where she got them, I don't know but it seems that the people who published them should do a little better job of proofreading! Here they are:

- "Next weekend's Fasting and Prayer Conference in Whitby Hall includes all meals."
- "Sunday morning sermon: Jesus Walks On The Water. Sunday evening sermon: Searching for Jesus."

- "Miss Charlene Mason sang 'I will not pass this way again,' giving obvious pleasure to the congregation."
- "Next Thursday there will be tryouts for the choir. They need all the help they can get."
- "At the evening service tonight, the sermon topic will be: 'What is Hell?' Come early and listen to our choir practice."
- "The ladies of the church have cast off clothing of every kind. They may be seen in the basement Friday afternoon."
- "This evening at 7 p.m. there will be a hymn singing in the park across from the church. Bring a blanket and come prepared to sin."
- "Low Self-Esteem Support Group will meet Thursday at 7 p.m. Please use the back door."
- "Weight Watchers will meet at 7 p.m. at the Assembly Hall. Please use the double door at the side entrance."

So, what more can I say except "go to church on Sunday instead of playing golf!" Also, keep a smile on your face, a song in your heart and don't sweat the little things in your life.

Not Seeking Sainthood – September 14, 2010

To the editor:

I have told your readers at one time or another about my entering the seminary with the possible intention of becoming a priest. Now I would like to tell you about a trip to church one Sunday and finding a bulletin with an article in it entitled "How does someone become a saint?" Needless to say, this caught my attention and I thought it was something I should pursue.

I learned that saints are people in heaven who lived lives of great charity and heroic virtue. The church believes that these people are worthy of imitation.

The article stated that there are three steps to becoming a recognized saint. "Venerable" is the title the pope gives someone who died after living a life of heroic virtue. Next, to be beatified and called "Blessed," a miracle has to be attributed to the candidate's intercession. Finally, to be canonized and recognized as a "saint," a second miracle is required.

WOW!

The last stipulation before being eligible for sainthood is death.

I think it was then, after due consideration of all the requirements for sainthood, that my enthusiasm for sainthood was dulled somewhat.

I came to the conclusion that I should continue my journey here on earth doing the things I can do best – take my remaining days, one day at a time, with a positive attitude, a smile on my face and not sweat the little things in my life. And say my daily prayers to my namesakes St. Joseph, St. Anthony and St. Herman for their guidance in my life.

Whatcha think?

Christmas Thoughts – December 23, 2010

To the editor:

In previous years, I used to write a lengthy Christmas letter to friends and relatives country-wide. My Christmas letter would bring everyone up to date on what was going on in Papa Joe's life. This used to be a lengthy dissertation but things aren't as busy as in the past.

I do continue to take my remaining days one day at a time, with a positive attitude, a smile on my face and I try not to sweat the little things in my life. And, I do continue to say my daily prayers, thanking God for all the wonderful things he has given me and done for me.

Then, as I used to do and I will do now for you, I gave everyone my holiday greeting and a few thoughts to ponder. Now, as the holiday season approaches, it's a good time to reflect on the true meaning of this wonderful season.

In one of my Christmas letters I suggested to my friends that this season is a good time to be thankful, and that we need to listen and we need to remember. Now I would like to pass these thoughts to you.

We need to take the time to be thankful for all the things that are precious to us. We need to thank God for all that He has done for us and the things that He has given us, especially our families, friends and good fortunes.

We need to take the time to listen. Listen to a child's laughter of innocence, listen to the bells that ring for prosperity, listen to birds that sing for love, listen to a prayer for strength and wisdom and most of all, listen to your heart.

We need to remember all the good times and things that have happened to us. Think of our freedom, good fortunes and all the people who made us who we are. Remember our youth (for we will never see it again) and help our children to achieve their dreams.

We need to remember those who cannot be with us to celebrate and especially those who are less fortunate than us. We need to strive to make this holiday season a time to reflect on the good news of the world and the simple joys that teach us not to forget, but to remember.

Those, my dear friends, are my words of wisdom. With them I send my love and very best wishes and I hope the good Lord has richly blessed you and yours. I pray that you have a healthy, happy, wonderful and joyful holiday season.

Friends – December 3, 2010

To the editor:

We recently celebrated Thanksgiving day. I hope our thoughts focused on the wonderful things in our lives that God has bestowed upon us.

I think I have more to be thankful for than most people because God has given me 86 years of pretty good health, a happy life, a positive attitude, a good sense of humor (I think) and the ability not to sweat all the little things in my life – most of the time.

Did you notice a little doubt sneaking in there? Well, I do have to admit I am no longer a spring chicken! There are some things God doesn't give us any control over – like wrinkles and gray hair (at least I still have some and gray is a beautiful color!) Or the bald spot on the back of my head (no big deal Papa Joe, you can't see it anyway) and the belt that bears a few expanding waist line marks. (I once asked the question, "does leather shrink?" but I never got an answer. I think I know what it is though.)

Yes, I jest a little, but in reality, most of us celebrate some type of a thanksgiving most days. It's a brief thanksgiving when we say our grace before our daily meals for the food we are about to eat and also giving thanks for some of the special things that have been bestowed upon us or one of our loved ones.

Thanks for my husband keeping his job. Thanks for my son graduating from high school. Thanks for my sister's successful operation. Thanks for that warm bed on a cold night. Thanks for that hug from your spouse, child or grandchild. A kiss on the cheek is even better and is certain to bring a flutter from the heart. And so on and so on. See what I mean? Every day can be a Thanksgiving day.

So while Thanksgiving day is over, I still want to thank each and every one of you for the friendship you have shared with me since I came to Midland on Groundhog Day, Feb. 2, 1948. I sincerely wish you good health, peace, hope and happiness.

May God always hold you in the palms of His hands.

The Answers – October 15, 2010

To the editor:

Recently, in an effort to get my ducks in a row, I have been concentrating on the consolidation and elimination of things I have been saving for the past hundred years – or so.

One of my latest projects is going through the boxes and boxes of photos I have taken of the give grandkids for the past 21 years. I'm trying to sort them out so I can send each kid his or her fair share. Boy, they'll really love seeing what they looked like as small kids.

As I look at their baby pictures I get carried away with their beauty and innocence. Then they grow up and go to high school. What a change in the personalities over the years.

The in-between years also includes words of misunderstanding, confusion, misinterpretation and so on. Whatever! Which brings me up to an old article I found that was supposedly children's science exam answers. I think you will enjoy them. See what you think.

Q: How is dew formed? A. The sun shines down on the leaves and makes them perspire.

Q: What happens to your body as you age? A. When you get old, so does your bowels and you get Continental.

Q: What happens to a boy when he reaches puberty? A. He says goodbye to his boyhood and looks forward to his adultery.

Q: Name a disease associated with cigarettes. A. Premature death.

Q: How are the main parts of the body categorized? (e.g. abdomen) A. The body is consisted into three parts – the brainium contains the brain, the borax contains the heart and lungs and the abdominal cavity contains the five bowels – A, E, I, O and U.

Q: What does "Varicose" mean? (I do like this one) A. Nearby

Q: What is a fibula? A. A small lie

Q: Give the meaning of the term "Cesarean Section." A. The Cesarean Section is a district in Rome.

Q: What does the word "benign" mean? A. Benign is what you will be after you be eight. Ugh!!!

There you be folks – whatcha think? I think you should think positive, with a smile on your face, take life one day at a time and for goodness sakes, don't sweat the little things in your life.

A Happier Place – November 9, 2010

To the editor:

Do you know that your funny bone is one of the most important bones in your body? The funny bone I'm talking about is the one that has to do with laughter. Laughter is a great stress buster because when we laugh, our breathing and heart rate increases and then, when they drop, we feel more relaxed.

If we combine laughter with physical activity or exercise, like walking each day, we can do wonders. This combination is like a euphoria for me and I find my whole attitude changes and I want to be "more giving" and do more for others. Maybe that's why I donate blood every eight weeks.

I try very, very hard to never forget that there are many more less fortunate people than me: the poor, terminal ill (including some of my closest and dearest friends) and many who are just alone and lonely.

I think we all need to touch more, hug more, kiss more and especially laugh more. When I have this loving and giving attitude toward others ,not only do I feel better, but more importantly, I find they feel happier and they even laugh more.

So, what I'm really trying to say is laugh, laugh, laugh! Even if your laugh is a cackle or you think you laugh too loud like Papa Joe does sometimes.

Laughter not only makes the quality of your life better, but being around you will be a happier place for others, who really need it. I also firmly believe that by adding humor and laughter to your lives, you will review life's problems with a different perspective and definitely eliminate a lot of its stresses.

Now, I want you all to do two things for me. First of all, go back and read the entire episode I have just written on laughter. Then think about it and let it settle in a minute. The second thing I want you to do for me is at the count of four, give Papa Joe a great big, from the stomach, hearty laugh! One, two three four ... Ha! Ha! Ha! Ha!

Papa Joe's Favorite Christmas Present – December 24, 2010

What was Papa Joe's life like as a kid at Christmas time in Indiana? And, what was my best ever Christmas present?

Christmas at my home was celebrated with my mother, four sisters, two brothers and me, the youngest, Joseph Herman Anthony.

As I remember, the Christmas tree in our home was put up the day before Christmas. I don't know if this was an old German custom of mom's or not.

About a week before Christmas, mom would close the front room and put newspapers all over the windows so us kids couldn't peek in from the outside.

Needless to say, all of us kids tried to peek in from time to time but to no avail. I do remember lying on my side one day trying to peek under the locked door and getting caught. Mom told me not to do that or Santa may not bring me any presents.

Sometime later that night as I was in the kitchen with my older sisters, there was a knock on the front door. One of my older sisters answered it and I heard a gruff voice say, "I'm one of Santa's helpers and you tell little Joe if he tries to peek again, Santa will bring him a bucket of coal instead of some presents."

(It wasn't until later years that I learned one of my brothers-in-law was Santa's helper that night.)

We didn't have electricity in our house back in the twenties, so naturally we didn't have electric lights for the tree. Instead, mom used small candles, placed on little 3-4 inch metal discs with a little clip which was used to attach them to the tree branches. Needless to say, only adults were allowed to light them.

After Santa ha come and left, mom would light the tree candles and there always was a fire in the fireplace o enhance the room. Then, the very anxious kids were allowed in the room for our presents. I say presents, but since we didn't have a dad and since mom didn't have any money, our presents consisted of the necessities of life: socks, underwear, shirts or some type of clothing. And one toy, a cap pistol or some kind of a kid's game.

However, the one Christmas and present I most vividly remember was the year Santa brought me a new leather jacket.

Boy, oh boy what a wonderful present – and it wasn't a hand-me-down! Being the youngest, I got a lot of hand-me-downs.

It wasn't a fancy or expensive jacket, but it was a leather jacket. Unfortunately, it was unlined and somewhat cold in the winter but I still wore it with pride. I still wore it months later even after it got a little small for me. Thanks again God, I mean Santa Claus, for the great gift!

Mom's final admonition, which I have never forgotten, was that Christmas is Christ's Day, and not just a day to get presents. Also, never write "X-MAS." In writing it this way, you are taking the Christ out of Christmas. Since it is Christ's birthday, let's make sure Christ stays in Christmas.

Merry Christmas.

Fuzzy Feelings – February 16, 2011

To the editor:

The month of February provides me with a yearly reminder that I started working for Dow Corning on Feb. 2, 1948, also known as Groundhog Day. February also has another special day for me, Valentine's Day, which we celebrated Monday.

Back in 1948, I was met and picked up at the Saginaw train station and delivered to Dow Corning to begin my wonderful 38-1/2 year career.

I did have some apprehension that day as we drove along the Tittabawassee River Road. Snow, ice, wilderness and cloudy. I'm sure Punxsutawney Phil didn't see his shadow that day!

The further we went, the more I started asking myself, "Joe, what did you get yourself into this time?" I was coming from southern Indiana, a relatively warm area in the winter. I hadn't seen that much snow since I was in Germany during WWII.

Then, as the driver came around a bend in the road and was approaching Dow Corning, there appeared a very large billboard sign advertising Champagne Velvet, "the beer with the million dollar flavor."

When I saw that sign I immediately perked up because CV was made in my home town of Terre Haute, Ind. "If they sell CV here, everything is going to be all right," I thought. It was! The billboard and CV are gone now, but I'm still here 63 years later!

Ah, good old memories.

Recently I was out shopping and Christmas was gone but Valentine's Day had made its entrance – cards, candy, hearts and the whole works.

So I got the fever and decided to beat the crowds and bought Valentine cards for all the children and grandchildren and candy hearts for some friends.

Valentine's Day, however, is a lot more than greeting cards and candy to me. In my mind, valentines are about people we love – past and present. The day is a reminder to me – and you – to remember all the valentines of our lives.

So even though Valentine's Day is past, don't forget to say "I love you" to your loved one. These are words that your spouse needs to hear to get him or her through the daily trials and tribulations of life. I believe you should put your spouse before everyone because they are your lifetime companion and should be honored.

But you also can call a few others you love and tell them "I love you," too. Who says you can't love more than one person – in different ways of course. So call your friends who might be lonely and tell them you're thinking of them. In fact, ask them out to lunch the next day. One of the most precious gifts you can give someone is your time.

If you're with a friend, give them the ultimate gift – a Papa Joe hug. That will give each of you a nice warm fuzzy feeling!

Finally don't forget to honor the Lord our God every day of your life in your prayers. And while you're at it, don't forget Papa Joe in your prayers because – "I love you!"

Love – January 28, 2011

To the editor:

It was four years ago in January when my beloved wife, Marjorie Rose, was taken to heaven to be with God and other members of her family. She is truly missed here at home.

The memory of my wife brought forth many thoughts of love so I have decided to write a few comments on that subject. It's something I think about and live for every day. Love is what makes the world go around.

We need to keep reminding those we love that we care about them, not only in times of emotional or physical needs but every time we talk to them. "I love you" is such a simple phrase, yet so many times we neglect to say it.

I have spoken to friends who say they have known the one true love of their lives and the lesson is always the same – life has to end but true love does not. Too often we take our loved ones for granted. When they are gone, we have to remember, it's for good. So we need to show them how much we love them before it's too late. Tell them often that you love them and are thankful and appreciative for their love.

I remember when one of my favorite comics, Haggar The Horrible, said, "We can all be rough and tough as nails, but sometimes we should be soft and tender with those we love." There's nothing wrong with letting our guard down once in a while and showing some affection occasionally.

You may be able to return a smile, but without love it's like trying to tell the wind what pain is. Love can be your child's first day of school. It only happens that one day but somehow it lasts forever.

A quote from years ago stated: "As you ramble on through life whatever be your goal, keep your eye on the doughnut and not the hold." What does it mean? My interpretation is that as we go through life we have to look at the overall picture and not just concentrate on one thing. We learn or realize that love comes in many size, shapes and forms.

Ann Landers once said, "Love is content with the present, it's hope for the future and it doesn't brood over the past. It's the day in and the day out chronology of irritations, problems, compromises, small disappointments, big victories and working toward a common goal."

If you have love in your life, it can make up for a great many things that are missing. If you don't, no matter what else there is, there is not enough!

Yes, I miss my wife's love and I am lonely, but when God intervenes and takes a loved one away from us, we have to learn to continue on with our life. I am learning to replace part of my wife's love from my children's and grandchildren's love.

My philosophy of life continues to be, "take life one day at a time with a positive attitude and a smile on your face and try not to sweat the little things."

Many years ago when my wife, Margie, went back to college for another degree she wrote this very profound statement, "Reach out – and love one another. Many people hide themselves behind a wall of illusion. They never glimpse the truth. Then it's too late and they pass away. With our love we could save the world. All we have to do is to realize it's all within ourselves – no one else can make us change. People who gain the world and lose their soul – they don't know, they can't see. Are you one of them?"

Pretty profound, eh? I think Margie was saying, "Tell everyone you love them."

A kiss and an embrace will mend hurt when it comes from deep inside of you. And, remember, spend some time with your loved ones, because they are not going to be around forever!

Words of Wisdom – May 24, 2011

To the editor:

I believe most readers are aware that one of my pleasures of life is when I'm out and about shopping I enjoy "meeting and greeting" strangers with a "Hi, how are you?" and with a smile.

There isn't much of a conversation but I sure get a lot of smiles from people. I also get some strange looks once in awhile!

Then there's the different atmosphere when I occasionally walk into my favorite watering hole and I'm greeted with "Hello Papa Joe, whatcha say?" One of my favorite responses is "Save your money and buy beer." Very profound, eh?

Or, "Hello Papa Joe, whatcha know?" To keep the rhyme going my general response generally is, "Ho, ho, I just got back from Kokomo!" or "Ho, ho, I just got back from Buffalo!" I prefer the latter because that's where my dear, sweet Marjorie Rose was born.

Really high level, intelligent greetings and responses, eh? Maybe not, but they sure generate a lot of smiles among the people in the immediate area. The really intelligent conversations and good fellowship take place when seated and sipping on a cold iced tea with several lemon slices – really! Or a nonalcoholic Budweiser draft (darn doctors).

Silly, eh! Maybe, but it's just one more learning experience as we ramble our way through life. You would be surprised how much you can learn sitting around a round table – or even a long table! Especially if those having the conversation have had a toddy or two.

I had a learning experience recently and I wasn't even expecting it. And I didn't even have a toddy! I was looking for something in my "stuff" drawer and couldn't find it. I learned I should start filing my "stuff" instead of just throwing it in a drawer!

Fortunately I did find something I think will be more interesting to you – some words of wisdom!

So, I'm passing them on for your enjoyment. Here goes …

I've Learned:

- That the good Lord didn't do it all in one day. What makes me think I can?
- That love, not time, heals all wounds.
- That everyone you meet deserves to be greeted with a smile.
- That no one is perfect until you fall in love with them.
- That I wish I could have told my wife that I love her one more time.
- That one should keep his words soft and tender, because tomorrow he may have to eat them.
- That when your newly-born child holds your little finger in his first, you're hooked for life.
- That life is like a roll of toilet paper – the closer it gets to the end, the faster it goes.
- And, as you make your journey through life, take it with a smile on your face, a song in your heart, one day at a time, with a positive attitude and don't sweat the little things.

A Wonderful Feeling – July 1, 2011

To the editor:

A couple of weeks ago on a Saturday morning, I decided to go out for a pizza lunch. As I was enjoying my lunch I noticed an elderly gray headed and bearded gentleman enter the restaurant carrying a can of soda pop. He purchased a single cellophane-wrapped chocolate cookie and then sat at a table by the window.

As I watched him, he started unwrapping his cookie as methodically as a surgeon preparing for an operation. He then started breaking off small pieces of the cookie and eating them one at a time – relishing each bite.

I continued to watch him as I quietly ate my pizza. About the time he was finishing eating his cookie and drinking his can of soda, I couldn't help but wonder what his status in life was, but it was not mine to presume. So, without hesitation, as he was gently rolling up his cookie wrapper to discard, I took a piece of my pizza on a paper napkin, approached him and offered it to the gentleman.

He accepted the pizza very graciously with a nice smile on his face. I went back to my table to finish my last piece of pizza and watch the nice gentleman as he methodically consumed his piece of pizza. I couldn't help but wonder how long it would take for the gentleman to consume an entire pizza, even the small one I had.

As I passed the gentleman on my way out, I said to him, "Have a nice day!" He in turn thanked me and said the pizza was delicious. I departed with a very uplifting feeling of well being!

Later that afternoon, I called one of my daughters and told her of my incident at the restaurant. She started laughing and said, "Dad, that's a random act of kindness." I told her I had probably done a lot of acts of kindness but I never knew they were called "random." Now I know – live and learn, Joe!

Anyway, the following Saturday I decided on another pizza luncheon. As I was enjoying my pizza, lo and behold, who should come into the restaurant but the same gentleman I had befriended the week before.

It was the same scenario, a can of soda, a chocolate cookie and a seat by the window. The same eating of the cookie, bite by bite and old Papa Joe giving him a slice of pizza to enjoy and our farewells. His only added comment this time was, "I hope it doesn't rain before I eat my pizza and get home."

I didn't think it was going to rain or I would have offered him a ride home. I don't know where home is, but I think the next time I see my friend, I will learn his name and offer him a ride home. Another act of kindness! God, I feel good just thinking about it!

And the story continues. I recently flew to Texas to help celebrate two of my grandchildrens' graduations. The Saturday after my return home, I decided on a pizza lunch and to see if my old friend might be there. He wasn't but the restaurant was packed full of young children in their soccer uniforms and several adult parents. They were enjoying the food as much as each other. When the food was done, they started in on a large cake and several packages of cookies.

As I was enjoying my pizza and the festivities, a very nice young lady approached my table and asked me if I would like a cookie. A very thoughtful gesture and I very willingly accepted the cookie with a wonderful feeling of appreciation.

It wasn't until later that I remembered I had visited the restaurant to give a "random act of kindness," but this time I had received one instead. "Give and ye shall receive." Or can we call it "a random act of kindness reciprocity."

Regardless of what they call it, it was a wonderful feeling. Now, please go forth with a smile on your face and a song in your heart with God's blessing. And don't forget to pass it on.

What To Do? – August 2, 2011

To the editor:

I was recently visiting my daughter in Texas and the graduation of a granddaughter from college and a grandson from high school. Since my daughter wouldn't let me do anything strenuous, I decided to write a letter to the editor – one of my enjoyments in life.

Occasionally I have tried to share how I developed my proclivity for letter writing. One supposition was that it happened in Sister Claudia's sixth grade classroom where quite frequently I was commissioned to write, a couple hundred times, "I must not talk in class!"

I don't know if it helped my yen for writing but I do think it helped my penmanship!

I have dozens of letters to the editor I have started but never finished. I guess I just couldn't come up with a happy ending. Many years ago I also started writing "A Letter of Love to My Grandchildren." Four hundred and some typewritten pages, but I still haven't put an ending on my book.

I started writing the book when the grandkids were very young. In fact, I don't believe one of them was born yet. My purpose in writing the book was to convey to them some of Grampa Joe's thoughts and recollections that they could read as they grew up. One such recollection was when my son last his longtime friend and companion, Spike, a golden lab.

I think Spike died of old age and went to doggie heaven. Since my son had Spike for many years and they became very close, he decided to give Spike a premium burial. He had Spike cremated and took his ashes and sprinkled them on their favorite duck hunting lake in Florida. I think I recall my son saying he took a couple of beers to make the celebration official.

The celebration of Spike's death got me to thinking and wondering if I should consider cremation on my demise and have my ashes spread on the Gulf at the foot of Second Street South in Naples, Fla., where I spent a lot of beach time with my friends. Great memories. I could keep an eye on my friends!

Then I had another idea I told the grandkids about. The idea was to have my ashes divided into three urns with each of my children getting an urn as a reminder of their father. But then I wondered, what if one of the children didn't want Dad's ashes lying around the house? I figured she or he could give the urn to the other sister or brother and then that child would have two thirds of Dad's ashes lying around the house.

One child would finally have all of Dad's ashes and it would be his or her responsibility to get rid of Dad. I wonder what they would do with the ashes? I bet they wouldn't be at the beach on Second Street South in Naples. Maybe curbside at 15 Brown Court in Midland?

P.S. Not to worry. I have talked to all my children and they have all agreed that when the time comes, Papa Joe should be and will be buried with the love of his life, Marjorie Rose. She has probably been wondering where I've been!

It's All About Grandparents – September 11, 2011

To the editor:

Regardless of how old you are today, you have talked about grandparents all of your life. But how did that come about? Well, listen up kids – I'm going to tell you the entire story!

The first Sunday after Labor Day isn't just a day to mourn the end of summer. It marks National Grandparents Day, a day set aside to honor grandparents and help children become aware of the benefit of having grandparents in their lives.

Grandparents Day was initiated by Marian Lucille Herndon McQuade, a West Virginia housewife with 15 children, 40 grandchildren and eight great-grandchildren. In 1970, McQuade sought to set aside a special day just for grandparents. After an intensive lobbying effort in 1973, West Virginia became the first state with a Grandparents Day. Originally held in May, the date was shifted to September because May was crowded with other holidays and because September would signify the "autumn years of life." It was proclaimed nationally by President Jimmy Carter in 1978 and observed nationwide for the first time in 1979.

Now, wasn't that interesting? Yes, but not as funny as some of those grandma and grandpa stories. Let's start in the bathroom where grandma was putting on her makeup under the watchful eyes of her young granddaughter as she had done many times before. After she had applied her lipstick and started to leave, the little one said, "But grandma, you forgot to kiss the toilet paper goodbye."

One time one of my grandkids asked me how old I was. I teasingly told him I wasn't sure. "Look in your underwear Papa Joe, mine says 4-6," he replied.

My grandparents are funny! When they bend over you hear gas leaks and they blame their dog!

My all-time favorite grandparent story is the one when the teacher told her first grade class to put their hands over their hearts for a pledge. Little Joe put his hand on his fanny. The teacher said, "That's not your heart, Joe." "Yes it is, teacher, because every time grandma picks me up she pats me there and says, 'Joe, bless your little heart.'"

Now, Papa Joe would be remiss if he didn't offer his words of wisdom about grandkids. I have wonderful grandchildren and I love them all. But, please God, let me remember that I have lived loved and enjoyed this life. Do not let me take away from their enjoyment by me complaining about every ache and pain. (Although I have earned them all!)

That way, in their later years, they will remember me with pleasure and say "I wish I had Papa Joe's genes. He never had anything wrong with him!"

God bless all of you wonderful grandparents.

Broken Proverbs – October 15 2011

To the editor:

I recently found an old yellowed Ann Landers column submitted by a fourth grade teacher. She gave her class the beginning of some well known proverbs and asked them to complete the saying. Hopefully you will enjoy some of them.

- It's always darkest ... just before you flunk a test.
- There is nothing new ... under a rock.
- A journey of a thousand miles begins with ... a private jet.
- A committee of three ... gets things done when they are not fighting.
- If you can't stand the heat ... try the Antarctic.
- Better late than ... absent.
- A rolling stone may ... dent the floor.
- If at first you don't succeed ... live with it.
- Laugh and the world laughs with you. Cry ... and then blow your nose.
- A bird in the hand is ... better than a woodpecker on your head.
- Early to bed, early to rise ... and you will get the best cereal.
- It is better to light a candle than ... to light a bomb.
- A miss is as good as ... a mister.
- A penny saved ... is not a lot.
- Don't burn your bridges ... or you'll fall in the lake.
- Haste makes ... sweat.

As long as we're talking about the fourth grade, I want to tell you about a Washington school district that tested students on their first aid knowledge and the "treatments" they came up with.

- For fainting, rub the person's chest or if it's a lady rub her arm above her hand.
- For fractures, see if the limb is broken – wiggle it gently back and forth.
- For nose bleeds, put the nose lower than the body.
- For snake bites, bleed the womb(sic) and rape(sic) the victim in a blanket for shock.
- For asphyxiation, apply artificial respiration until patient is dead.

Wow! I think we had better move those fourth-graders up a grade or two! Oh well, just don't sweat the little things in your life and think positive.

A Week of Birthdays – October 29, 2011

To the editor:

First of all, thanks to all of the kind and thoughtful people who sent me a birthday card. Special thanks to the Midland Daily News for the birthday announcement in the October 19 issue of the paper even though you neglected to mention that my birthday was October 20.

No problem though. If I was congratulated personally on the 19th, I merely replied, "Thanks, but my birthday is on October 20th." On Friday, October 21, everything was pretty well straightened out and we had forgotten my October 20 birth. But, wait a minute, another announcement showed up on Saturday, October 22 announcing my birthday was October 20. Whoops again.

Folks officially my birthday was on October 20, but I really don't care. I sure had a lot of fun, smiles, laughs and "Happy Birthday Papa Joes." It was an entire week of "birthdays."

The great news is that the California preacher who predicted the world would be obliterated on October 21 was wrong. I knew that wouldn't happen, as did all of you, because nobody sent me all of their gold, silver, and jewelry.

So, all's well that ends well! Now we can all meet at our favorite "pub" and give a toast to our real benefactor – thank you kind and gentle God! Now we will have more days to pray and be thankful for everything He gives us, day after day.

Life Lessons – 2011

To the editor:

As I have rambled on through this wonderful life of mine, I have learned and enjoyed many wonderful things. I have not achieved the status of rocket scientist yet, but I'm still working on it, step by step. Please follow my lead by taking your life one day at a time with a positive attitude and I'm sure you will learn and enjoy a lot of wonderful things, like some of these.

I've learned:

- That no matter how much I care, some people just don't care back.
- That it's not what you have in your life but who you have in your life that counts.
- That you shouldn't compare yourself to the best others can do.
- That two people can look at the exact same thing and see something totally different.
- That your family won't always be there for you. It may seem funny but people you aren't related to can take care of you and love you and teach you to trust people again.
- That heroes are the people who do what needs to be done when it needs to be done, regardless of the consequences.
- That you either control your attitude or it controls you.
- That you can keep on going long after you think you can't.
- That sometimes when I'm angry, I have the right to be angry, but that doesn't give me the right to be cruel.
- That the people you care about most in life are taken from you, too.

May God bless you and always keep you in the palm of His hands.

Home Remedies – January 26, 2012

To the editor:

Did you ever stop to think that there are probably as many home remedies as there are modern remedies? And the important thing is they don't cost a bundle of money. Back in January 2006, I witnessed a band of nomads passing through Naples, Fla. They were passing out simple home remedies for a minor contribution.

Luckily I obtained a few of those home remedies and I would like to pass them on for your pleasure. But, remember, do not take any of them seriously.

AMAZING SIMPLE HOME REMEDIES:

- If you are choking on an ice cube, don't panic. Simply pour a cup of boiling water down your throat and presto, the blockage will be almost instantly removed.
- Clumsy? Avoid cutting yourself while slicing vegetables by getting someone else to hold them while you chop away.
- Avoid arguments with your wife about lifting the toilet seat by simply going outside behind the garage.

- For high blood pressure sufferers, simply cut yourself and bleed for a few minutes, thus reducing the pressure in your veins. Remember to use a timer.
- A mouse trap placed on top of your alarm clock will prevent you from rolling over and going back to sleep after you hit the snooze button.
- If you have a bad cough, take a large dose of laxatives. Then you will be afraid to cough.
- Have a bad toothache? Smash your thumb with a hammer and you will forget the toothache.
- Sometimes we just have to remember what the rules of life really are. You only need two tools: WD 40 and duct tape. If it doesn't move and it should, use the WD 40. If it shouldn't move and it does, use the duct tape.

And, finally, be really nice to your family and friends because you never know when you might need them to empty your bed pan.

May God keep you in the palm of his hand and healthy (without the need for any amazingly simple home remedies).

Hug Therapy – May 8, 2012

To the editor:

I once read an article in the Alzheimer Support Network News. A quick into to the article was that touch is not only very ice, but very needed! Scientific research supports the theory that stimulation by touch is absolutely necessary for our physical as well as our emotional well-being.

Various experiments have shown that touch can make us feel better about ourselves and our surroundings and can cause measurable physiological changes in the toucher and the touched.

We are just beginning to understand the power of touch. While there are many forms of touching, it is suggested that hugging is a very special one that can contribute in a major way to healing and health.

No, I have not forgotten my hugging enthusiasm; it just seems like there are always too many things to do. But as I requested in a letter many years ago, I am requesting that readers take the time today to give someone a hug.

How about right now?

Who is the nearest person to you? Approach that person with a nice smile on your face and say, "I need a hug."

Surprise! Didn't that feel nice and give you a warm, fuzzy feeling? A hug is of no value until it is given away, so give it away as soon as you can.

One last comment: If you see Papa Joe out and about and would like a hug, I am more than happy to oblige. I can always use an extra hug or two myself.

Over the Hill – January 20, 2012

To the editor:

I was going to tell readers that they should avoid getting old or the youngsters will make fun of them and call them "over the hill." But you know what? I don't mind being "over the hill" because it's better than being "six feet under."

That brings up a good question: How can you tell if you're over the hill? My friend Digger O'Dell shared these answers with me.

- You no longer laugh at Preparation H commercials.
- Your arms are almost too short to read the newspaper.
- The only reason you're still awake at 2 a.m. is indigestion.
- People ask what color your hair used to be.
- You enjoy watching the news.
- You no longer think of speed limits as a challenge.
- You have dreams about prunes.

- You browse the bran section in the grocery store.
- You start worrying when your supply of Ben Gay is low.
- You think a CD is a certificate of deposit.
- You have more than two pairs of glasses.
- You read the obituaries daily.
- You enjoy hearing about other people's operations.
- You know all the warning signs of a heart attack.

If any of the above apply to any of you, I hate to tell you, but you are over the hill.

Irish Humor – March 16, 2012

To the editor:

St. Patrick's Day is forthcoming but what can I tell you historically that I haven't already told you in the past? I can repeat that old myth that there were snakes in Ireland. Just a rumor! Some of the Irish laddies just drank too much and thought they were seeing snakes. However, the snakes were all gone the next morning after the laddies sobered up.

I think I told you the story about the Irishman who drank too much, fell into a vat of Guinness and drowned. He did get out of the vat twice to relieve himself before he drowned.

I'm not much of a joke man but I did hear a couple recently, so I'm passing them on to you. Hope you enjoy them.

An Irishman, Englishman and Scotsman go into a pub and each order a pint of Guinness. Just as the bartender hands them over, three flies buzz down and one lands in each of the pints.

The Englishman looks disgusted, pushes his pint away and demands another.

The Scotsman picks out the fly, shrugs and takes a long swallow.

The Irishman reaches into the glass, pinches the fly between his fingers and shakes him while yelling, "Spit it out! Spit it out!"

A drunk staggers into a Catholic Church and enters a confession box, sits down and says nothing. The priest coughs a couple of times to get his attention but the drunk just sits. Finally, the priest pounds three times on the wall. The drunk mumbles, "ain't no use knocking, there's no paper on this side either."

Mary Clancy goes up to Father O'Grady after his Sunday morning message and she's in tears. He says, "So what's bothering you, Mary, my dear?"

She says, "Oh Father, I've got some terrible news. My husband passed away last night."

The priest says, "Oh Mary, that's terrible. Tell me, did he have any last requests?

"That he did, father..."

The priest asks, "What did he ask Mary?"

"He said, 'Please Mary put down that gun!'"

Just one final question: Do you know how the Irish jib got started? Too much to drink and not enough toilets!

God be with you as we celebrate this day of corned beef and cabbage and keep a smile on your face in honor of St. Pat and St. Joe.

Why Go to Church? – March, 2012

To the editor:

I received a nice letter recently from my good old D.C. buddy, The Rock, who said he has been working hard in The Villages in Florida. I was afraid to ask him, doing what?

Rock told me if I was spiritually alive, I would love his letter. If I am spiritually dead, I won't read it. If I am spiritually curious, there would still be hope for me. I think Mr. Rock knows this old seminarian's answer, but the question he put forth was: Why go to church?

A churchgoer wrote a letter to the editor of the newspaper and complained that it made no sense to go to church every Sunday.

"I've gone for 30 years now," he wrote, "and in that time I have heard something like 3,000 sermons. But for the life of me, I can't remember a single one of them. So, I think I'm wasting my time and the pastors are wasting their time by giving sermons at all."

This started a real controversy in the "Letter to the Editor" column, much to the delight of the editor. It went on for weeks until someone wrote this clincher: "I've been married for 30 years now. In that time my wife has cooked some 32,000 meals. But, for the life of me, I cannot recall the entire menu for a single one of those meals.

"But I do know this. They all nourished me and gave me the strength I needed to do my work. If my wife had not given me those meals, I would be physically dead today. Likewise, if I had not gone to church for nourishment, I would be spiritually dead today!"

When you are down to nothing...God is up to something! Faith sees the invisible, believes the incredible and receives the impossible! Thank God for our physical and our spiritual nourishment!

Thanks for the reminder, Rock; see you in church Sunday.

Healing Came from Forgiving and Forgetting – June 17, 2012

To the editor:

What's my next letter to the editor? Father's Day! But as you know, I am not a firm believer nor advocate of Father's Day. Why? You've been told before. I had a father but I never had a dad. There is a difference – a big, big difference.

Just a very brief explanation – if one can explain such a situation. I was the last of eight children and when I was about two years old, my father deserted my mother and her eight children! That was a pretty unbelievable thing to handle in the Depression years – the 1920s-30s.

Now for the purpose of this letter. My mother, father, brothers and sisters are all dead now – only Papa Joe the baby is left.

I have tried to reason why for years and years to no avail. Forgive and forget? Yep, I didn't have a dad for many years but thanks to a wonderful mother, brother and sisters, I have had a pretty good life.

Thank you God – forgive my father!

Today, I received the attached letter from a dear friend of mine, who also did not have a dad as a child. Yes, I often cried myself to sleep. Good night God!

The Absentee Father

I am not the way I used to be
I am stronger and wiser as you can see;
Remember my words, my father said,
As he cradled me up and laid me to bed;
You will someday be a man with a life of your own
With someone to love you as I have shown;
I will always be here to lend a hand
To help you and guide you when you don't understand;
Although I believed his words, I'd come to see
He was not the father he promised to be;
Instead he was a man that did not care
My mother was my father after he was not there;
He became a man free to roam
Not worrying of his family, or coming home;
Never a sports achievement nor first did he see
Neighborhood dads tried to include me;
I often cried myself to sleep
My father's love was not mine to keep;

I still miss my father I won't lie
Not a single hug or one last goodbye;
He walked out of my life and never turned my way
Oh why daddy … why didn't you stay?
-    Source unknown

Old Jokes Versus New Jokes – May 7, 2012

To the editor:

   I don't know if it's my imagination or old age but I'm beginning to think some of my old jokes are funnier than the newer ones. I got out some of my old Gems of the Day and want to pass them on to you for your readers' edification. (Folks, that means to enlighten – I'm just showing off my knowledge about one of the three big words I know!)

   Now folks, I'm going to run an opinion poll which I've never done before. Do you think these old "Gems" are funnier than today's jokes? Drop old Papa Joe a note at 15 Brown Court and give me your opinion. If worthwhile, I'll publish the results. Now, here's those "Gems" – enjoy.

- Have you noticed that very few people go the doctor when they have a bad cough or cold? They go to the theater or a concert and sit next to you.
- One of the best tests of religion is when you find yourself in church with nothing smaller than a $20 bill.
- My parents had a tough time getting married. Mom wouldn't marry him when he was drunk, and he didn't want to marry her when he was sober.
- Christmas is the season when you buy this year's gifts with next year's money.
- What is the best thing to do when the brakes fail while you are going downhill? Answer: Hit something cheap.
- Help a man when he is in trouble, and you can be sure he will remember you – when he is in trouble again.
- I knew I needed glasses the day I tried to dial the pencil sharpener.
- Things to do tomorrow: 1. Get up at the crack of dawn. 2. Stuff up the crack. 3. Go back to bed.

Happy laughing.

Problematic – July 2012

To the editor:

   Some time ago, I wrote a letter on home remedies that was very well received by readers. Today I'm going to give readers a series of problems without solutions. Some of them have been around the circuit before, but there are a few innovative questions to titillate the consciousness. Enjoy!

1. If a word is misspelled in the dictionary, how would we ever know?
2. If Webster wrote the first dictionary, where did he find the words?
3. Why do we sing "Take me out to the ball game" when we are already there?
4. Why is it called "after dark" when it really is "after light?"
5. Doesn't "expecting the unexpected" make the unexpected expected?
6. If all the world is a stage, where is the audience sitting?
7. If love is blind why is lingerie so popular?
8. Why is bra singular and panties plural?
9. How come abbreviated is such a long word?
10. Why do we wash bath towels? Aren't we clean when we use them?

Thanks to Traverse John for sending me the above nine years ago.

Bible of Living – August 17, 2012

To the editor:

This is an excerpt of an article from my book, "A Letter of Love to my Grandkids," that I started writing in 1993. Be prepared. I intend to send in some other excerpts from my book in the future. I'm pretty positive readers will enjoy them. What better way to start off than with my "Bible of Living." Enjoy.

In the last chapter of my book, I gave you some proverbs and quotes, some of which were pretty profound. I also told you I had some quotes, sayings, comments, observations or whatever you want to call them that I have collected over the past year or so. I jotted down this "Bible of Living" as I heard them, read them or thought of them. Now it is time to get this wealth of knowledge out to you so you can begin to use this information to make you more perfect human beings. At least I am sure they will make your life more fulfilling and living much more enjoyable. So whatcha say – ready to give it a chance? You may even want to copy them down, post them on your fridge or mirror and look at them periodically.

"BIBLE OF LIVING"

- See fun in everything you do.
- Laugh the loudest when the joke is on you.
- The secret of long life is being needed and doing something useful.
- Don't probe the shadows of your past life – let the past be in the past. Look in one direction only – ahead.
- Don't have regrets. Regrets imply sorrow. Each event is a learning experience.
- You should never grow old. You should just grow and grow until you leave this earth. You start all over many times in your life.
- Build people up – never tear them down. Especially, never say harsh things to your children – they will remember. They can't leave – they're too young – they have to take what you give out.
- Do the best you can with what you have. Make the most from the least.
- Don't give me flowers for my grave. Give me my love now and I'll give my love, too. You can't do anything for the dead. Be good to people while they are living.
- Learn how to fix things. Learn how to take care of yourself. Be independent – learn how to solve your own problems.
- Family background and what you have accomplished is history and it is important. You don't want to forget or lose your history. It is like losing part of your life.
- Make life better for those around you.
- If you worked hard enough and long enough you can accomplish just about anything.
- As long as you can see each day as a chance for something new to happen, you will stay young.
- Don't be afraid to say, "I Love You." Say it again and again and again. They are the sweetest words in the world.
- Love is caring about the other person's feelings almost as much as caring about your own.
- Care about yourself and be positive – "I Like Me. I am a good person."

Putting a Smile on Your Face – September 23, 2012

To the editor:

Where does all the time go? Recently I attended a retiree club party. Yes, there were a few strange looking faces. In fact, I was a little embarrassed when one guy asked me who I was. Come on Jerry, I haven't aged that much. Although I was one of the club's organizers 25 years ago. Where does all the time go?

Anyway, the thing that made my visit most enjoyable was the large number of friends who told me how much they thoroughly enjoyed my letters to the editor and to keep writing them. (Why do you think I'm writing this "thank you" letter?)

I am always amazed by the number of people who know me and always comment positively about my letters. I have received one complaint in all the years of my letter writing. I wasn't worried though – what did that guy know anyway?

So this is a "thank you" letter. Thank you. I also want to thank God while I'm at it for all the wonderful things he has done for me and does it on a daily schedule. God has especially given me the "power" to love everyone and be happy. This helps make letter writing easier.

I thoroughly enjoy writing my letters and primarily write them to put a smile on your face. Thanks a million to all my wonderful friends for telling me how important my letters are to you. Keep telling me that and I'll keep writing them. Thank you.

Love and Peace.

Getting Serious: Papa Joe Seeks Funding Support for Alzheimer's Association – September 13, 2012

To the editor:

Hi, this is Papa Joe writing another editorial. However, this is not going to be one of my humorous dissertations. This article is a serious plea for a tax free contribution for an extremely worthy organization, the Alzheimer's Association.

This year's "Walk To End Alzheimer's" will be at Emerson Park on Saturday, September 22 – act.alz.org/Midland – with registration at 9 a.m. and the opening ceremony and walk at 10 a.m. For more information, call 800-272-3900. Here is what they're up against and why we must contribute to find a cause and a cure for Alzheimer's:

- More than 5.4 million Americans are living with Alzheimer's Disease; more than 24,000 in Central Michigan.
- Every 69 seconds someone develops Alzheimer's Disease.
- Over 500,000 Americans suffer from younger-onset dementia (diagnosed before age 65).
- If nothing is done, 10 million Americans will develop Alzheimer's disease by 2050.
- 14.5 million Americans are caring for someone with dementia.

No, they cannot predict who will fall prey to the devastating disease, but we do know we are all at risk. It is not a pleasant feeling knowing we all can be affected with that horrible disease and can't do anything to prevent it, except help pay for research to find the cause and a cure.

It's All in Your Outlook – September 26, 2012

To the editor:

There is an old cliché that says, "We get old too soon and smart too late." I take solace in the fact that even though I am aging too fast, I think I am getting a little wise in the process.

Now, as for my contribution to society, I would like to impart some wisdom for your edification. If we're honest, we have to accept the fact that some of us are not the brightest individuals in the world. So, we have to be willing to accept the fact that there are many things in this life we can still learn.

First of all there are still a lot of us running through life so fast that often we are somewhat confused and really don't know what's going on in our life. Remember another cliché, "We don't take enough time to smell the roses."

We all need to, and have to, relax and enjoy the day! Sometimes we spend too much time thinking about the past and we worry about the negative things that have happened.

Why? There's not a darn thing we can do about how bad things were or all the bad things that have happened to us. Forget the past! Don't even think about it unless it is some good and wonderful thing that has happened to you. You can enjoy that thought momentarily and then forget about it and start dwelling on today!

Also, do not waste your time or energy thinking about the future. What will be, will be and you probably won't have any control over most of the things that are going to happen. So why worry about the unknowns? Besides, 95 percent of the things we worry about never happen.

Researchers examined the emotional content of some 180 autobiographies written by sisters at Notre Dame. The same nuns whose medical histories and other records are providing data on aging and disease.

By looking for key words such as "joy," "content," "happy," "love" and "hopeful," researchers found that those sisters with a strong positive outlook lived up to 10 years longer than those with less positive outlooks. Certainly nothing trivial about that, now is there?

Ralph Waldo Emerson once said, "What lies behind us and what lies before us are tiny matters compared to what lies within us." I think what he was trying to say is that there are a lot of wonderful things that are just waiting to be accomplished by us – right now – so what are we waiting for? Do it now! Get going!

Too often we put off until tomorrow and we make all those promises to ourselves concerning the wonderful things we are going to do, but unfortunately tomorrow never comes.

We have to be thankful for everything we have. I thank God every morning, noon and night for all the wonderful things he has given me and done for me in my long and illustrious life. Yes, there have been some very bump roads in my life, but I try not to swell on them – only the good things that have happened to me.

As Bing Crosby used to croon in one of his very popular songs, many years ago, "You have to accentuate the positive and eliminate the negative." Think negative and things will get much better. Thus the key word in my vocabulary is "positivity."

We Have a Lot to be Thankful For – November 18, 2012

To the editor:

Thanksgiving Day – the day we give thanks for all the good things of the past year. Why do we only pick one day out of the 365 days to give thanks? Our lives are so full of good things, we should have our own little thanksgiving every day.

We need to take the time daily for all the good things that are precious to us. We need to thank God for all he has done for us and the things he has given us, especially our families, friends and good fortunes. No, don't feel sorry for yourself. Just look around and you'll realize how fortunate you really are.

We need to take the time to listen and be thankful for a child's laughter of innocence, listen to the bells that ring for prosperity, listen to the birds that sing for joy and listen to a prayer for strength and wisdom and most of all listen to our heart.

We need to remember and be thankful for all the good times and things that have happened to us. Thankful for our freedom, good fortunes and all the people who made us who we are. Remember our youth (for we will never see it again) and help our children and their children achieve their dreams.

We need to remember to be thankful for those who cannot be with us. To help those who are less fortunate than us.

A positive attitude has helped me realize how fortunate I am and the many things I have to be thankful for. I am especially thankful that God has given me 88 years of healthy, happy life and a good sense of humor (I think) and the ability to not sweat the little things, while I have a smile on my face – most of the time!

So dear friends, I wish the same good fortune for all of you and your families. I especially want to thank all of you for the friendship you have shared with me over the years. I wish you good health, peace and happiness and hope you have a wonderful Thanksgiving Day with your loving family.

One final wish to you all.

May your stuffing be tasty, may your turkey be plump,

May your potatoes n' gravy have nary a lump,

May your yams be delicious, may your pies take the prize,

May your Thanksgiving dinner stay off your thighs.

One Day at a Time – October 2012

To the editor:

One of my many philosophies is to take life "one day at a time." Remember? Yesterday is history, tomorrow is a mystery, but today is the present – a gift from God! It's like every day is your birthday – you get the gift of life every day.

Let me tell you a story I read about an elderly, well-poised and proud man who is fully dressed each morning by eight o'clock, with his hair fashionably combed and shaved perfectly, even though he is legally blind.

His wife had passed away several months ago, making it necessary to move into a nursing home. As he was maneuvering his way to the elevator and being ushered to his new home, the administrator was providing him with a visual description of his tiny room. "I love it," he said. "Mr. Jones, you haven't seen the other room yet – just wait."

"That doesn't have anything to do with it," he replied. "Happiness is something you decide on ahead of time. Whether I like the room or not doesn't depend on how the furniture is arranged – it's how I arrange it in my mind. I have already decided to love it. It's like a decision I make every morning when I wake up. I have a choice – I can spend the day in bed recounting the difficulty I have with the parts of my body that no longer work or get out of bed and be thankful for the ones that do."

What a wonderful example for all of us, eh? Each day is a gift from God and we should focus on all the happy memories we have stored away in our minds. I am learning that old age is like a bank account. You can withdraw from it what you have put in it. So my advice to all of you would be to deposit a lot of happiness in your bank of memories for future withdrawals.

I would also suggest you start today because if you don't, you are losing some of the happiest times in your life for future reference. Think positive and, please, don't sweat the little things. May God smile on your today – and tomorrow – and the next day.

Happiness Comes from Giving, Not Getting – October 14, 2012

To the editor:

One would think with all the books on happiness, we would be the happiest generation ever. I once saw a book for sale titled, "How to be Happy Without Money." It cost $19.95, which means, I guess, that if you don't have any money, you can't even be happy without it!

Mort Crim once said, "We don't need books to explain the formula for happiness. Happiness is something that happens while we're thinking about something else."

What happy people have discovered is that happiness comes only as a result, not a goal. It's the result of doing things for others. Happiness results from giving, not getting!

When I am out and about with friends, I get very happy and want to tell jokes to everyone who will listen. When I tell my jokes, and they laugh, I laugh even harder.

I guess God has always told me, "Be happy, Joe." Where have you heard, "Take life one day at a time, with a positive attitude, and don't sweat the little things?" So be happy, enjoy life and especially everyone in it.

I think I was put on this earth to make people happy. At least grin! We all need love in our lives and making people laugh makes me happy, one of my loves in my life.

So today's thought can be this: "The way to happiness and a good enjoyable life is to have a good sense of humor." Smile! Remember, those who spread happiness to others can't escape it. Smile!

Doing for ourselves can be fun and bring pleasure and satisfaction. But that emotional high we call happiness results only from giving and not getting. As I said earlier, happy people have discovered that happiness comes only as a result, not a goal. It's the result of doing good things for others.

God bless you – and be happy.

Extensions – December 5, 2012

To the editor:

Recently, when I celebrated my 88th birthday, I was in a very joyful mood. I don't think the ginger ale my friends were feeding me had anything to do with it! As I have advanced through the years, I have enjoyed more and more all the wonderful experiences. I wonder how many more are out there just waiting for Papa Joe to experience? What do you think? Can I pull off the following?

Dear Lord, I have turned 88, but there are still places to dine, so I hope you'll let me live to 89.

Dear Lord, I'm still not ready to go, so do you think I could stay around for that nine-0?

Yes, there's still a lot I haven't done, so I hope you let me stick around until I'm 91.

No, I'm not finished yet with all I want to do, so would you please let me stay until I'm 92?

So many places I want to go, so very much to see, think you could manage to let me make it to 93?

The world is changing very fast and there is so much in store that I really would like to live to 94.

And if by then, by your good grace, I'm still alive, I'd like to stay just one more year, until I'm 95.

Many new gadgets will be here, with less and less to fix, which makes this a world I'd like to see when I turn 96.

I know, dear Lord, it might be nice in Heaven, but really I'd rather stay here until I'm 97.

By then I won't be very fast and sometimes will be late, but still it would be pleasant to be around at 98.

I really would like to see those great-grandkids of mine, so how about it, Lord, can I make it to 99?

One more year, dear Lord, is sure to be fun, could I please live to be 99 plus one?

Beyond that point, Lord, I have no requests, I know when you decide it's right, you'll give me the final test. Amen!

OK, dear Lord, take me when you're ready!

Thoughts About January as We Begin a New Year – January 3, 2013

To the editor:

I found this New Year's January poem in my old file. I don't remember if I wrote it or not, but I think it is worth sharing with readers. I hope you all enjoy it.

January

'Twas the month after Christmas and all through the house,
Nothing would fit me, not even a blouse.
The cookies I'd nibbled, and the nog I'd tasted
They all had gone to my waist.
When I got on the scale there was such a thunder
And I screamed when I looked at the number.
So, the last bits of food that I have must be banished
Because all the additional ounces still haven't vanished.
I won't have hot biscuits, cornbread or pie,
I'll munch on a carrot and quietly cry.
I'm hungry, I'm lonesome and life is a bore.
But isn't that what January is for?
Happy New Year!

Hug a Lot – January 31, 2013

To the editor:

It has been quite awhile since I have written a letter on hugging. One reason is I'm not getting my share – of hugs that is! So, dear friends, this is another reminder to get your arm muscles ready for action.

First and foremost, a few comments to make sure everything is done properly. Always make sure you have permission before giving a hug. Often, permission to hug is implicit in a relationship. Your sweetheart or close friends probably welcome a hug almost any time. However, you still need to respect people's need for privacy and space. Now, since all of you are my friends, you are welcome to give me a hug at any time. All you need to say is, "Papa Joe, I sure would like a big hug, will you please make me happy?" Get the message?

Now here are the whys and wherefores of hugging:

"Hugging is healthy. It helps the body's immune system, it keeps you healthier, it cures depression, it reduces stress, it induces sleep, it's invigorating, it's rejuvenating, it has no unpleasant side effects and hugging is nothing less than a miracle drug.

Hugging is all nature. It is organic, naturally sweet, no pesticides, no preservatives, no artificial ingredients and 100 percent wholesome.

Hugging is practically perfect. There are no movable parts, no batteries to wear out, no periodic checkups, low energy consumption, high energy yield, inflation proof, non-fattening, no monthly payment, no insurance requirements, theft-proof, non-taxable, non-polluting and, of course, fully returnable."

There you are, what more can I tell you? I've given you all the facts and figures so the rest is up to you. Give all those hugs to your friends and loved ones. Oh, and don't forget Papa Joe.

Say to me, "Papa Joe, you need a hug," and watch the big smile come to my face and probably your face as well as I give you a hug in return. We will both be smiling and very, very happy. Keep on hugging!

P.S. These hug thoughts are dedicated to a sweet old lady hugger friend I met at Hillcrest Adult Foster Care. Here's to you, Ziola! I'm saving a hug for you the next time I visit!

Sharing – January 17, 2013

To the editor:

Some time ago, I mentioned that I was going to start sharing some excerpts from my book, Letter of Love to My Grandkids." Naturally, I forgot. But today I read the book and found a little dissertation about my first television experience. Ah, the good old days!

This story goes back to the 1950s when my wife and I didn't have a television. Boy, that's archaic, isn't it? But Bud, who lived across the street, had one, and since Bud and his wife Angie were good friends of ours, they would often ask us to come over after we put the kids to bed. This was generally on Friday, Saturday or Sunday nights, the only times there were any decent programs on TV. Margie and I didn't really care what was on because just "seeing TV" was a big thrill in those days.

So on the nights we received an invitation, we would try to bathe the kids and get them to bed as early as we could so we could go across the street to Bud and Angie's to watch TV. After everyone was sound asleep, we could turn off all the lights except for the dining room light, because that was the window we could see from across the street. If any of the kids got up and came down the stairs, we would see them.

During each commercial break (yes they had commercials back then), we would go to Bud's front window and see if any of the kids were awake. If not, we would watch TV until a break in between programs, at which time I would run across the street to home and make sure everything was OK.

What a way to watch TV, eh?

But in retrospect, I don't remember ever having any problems with our kids getting up while we were over there. They were a lot like most little kids – they played hard and went to bed and slept through the night. Since they didn't have any TV to watch, and didn't have anything else to do, they went to bed without argument.

Do you know when we got our first TV? Unfortunately, it was the year Margie's mother died in Ft. Lauderdale, Fla. They had to get rid of the estate, so everything was either sold or given away – except for the TV. Since we didn't have one, everyone decided to ship it back to Midland for the Lubbehusens. So, that's how we got our first TV. I don't remember exactly how long it took for that TV to get to Midland, but at the time, in anticipation of getting a TV, it seemed like it took a year to arrive.

See how lucky we are today? If the TV goes off for five minutes, we panic and complain. Think about this story as one example of how much we should be very, very thankful for everything that we have.

Thank you, God, for everything you have done for me.

Too Many People Take Things for Granted – February 2013

To the editor:

Too often we take things for granted. Too often we forget to say thanks. Please let me share with you a very interesting story that a dear friend sent to me several years ago. It has an important message in it that I hope and pray you put into your daily life. I promise you, you will never regret it.

A newly arrived soul in Heaven was met by St. Peter. St. Peter and the soul took a tour around Heaven. They walked side-by-side inside a large workroom filled with angels.

St. Peter stopped in front of the first section and said, "This is the Receiving Section. Here, all petition to God said in prayers are received." The soul looked at the section, and it was terribly busy with so many angels sorting out petitions written on paper sheets and scraps from people all over the world.

They continued on until they reached the second section. St. Peter told the soul, "This is the Packaging and Delivery Section. Here, the graces and blessings the people asked for are processed and delivered to the living persons who asked for them." The soul noted again how busy I was. There were many angels working hard at that station, since so many blessings had been requested and were being packaged for delivery to Earth.

Finally, in the farthest corner of the room, the soul stopped at a very small station. To the surprise of the soul, only one angel was seated there, idly doing nothing. "This is the Acknowledgment Section," St. Peter told the soul.

"How is it that there's no work here?"

"So sad," St. Peter sighed. "After people receive the blessings they asked for, very few send acknowledgements."

"How does one acknowledge God's blessings?"

"Simple," St. Peter answered. "Just say, 'Thank you, Lord.'"

Attention Acknowledgement Section: Thank you, Lord! Thank you for giving me the ability to share this message and for giving me so many wonderful people here in Midland to share it with.

Have a good day, count your blessings and, if you want, I suggest you pass this along to remind everyone about how truly blessed we are.

Little Things – February 15, 2013

To the editor:

I often preach, "Don't sweat the little things in your life," because 95 percent are little – but sometimes those little things can mean the difference between life and death. And those little things can boil down to minutes, even seconds. Let me pass on a true story that illustrates my words of wisdom.

After the Sept. 11 attack on the Twin Towers, one company invited the members of other firms that had been decimated by the attack to share their available office space. At a morning meeting, the head of security told real stories about why many of the company's people were still alive and all the stories were just: Little Things.

As you might know, the head of the company got in late that day because his son started kindergarten. Another fellow was alive because it was his turn to bring donuts.

One woman was late because her alarm clock didn't go off in time.

One was late because of being stuck on the NJ Turnpike because of an auto accident.

One person missed his bus.

One spilled food on her clothes and had to take time to change.

One person's car wouldn't start.

One went back to answer the telephone.

One had a child that dawdled and didn't get ready as soon as he should have.

One couldn't get a taxi.

The one that struck me was the man who put on a new pair of shoes that morning, took the various means to get to work but before he got there, he developed a blister on his foot. He stopped at a drugstore to buy a Band-Aid. That is why he is alive today.

Now when Ii am stuck in traffic, miss an elevator, turn back to answer a ringing telephone ... all the little things that annoy me, I think to myself this is exactly where God wants me to be at this very moment.

The next time your morning seems to be going wrong, the children are slow getting dressed, you can't seem to find the car keys, you hit every traffic light, don't get mad or frustrated. God is at work watching over you.

May God continue to bless you wish all those annoying little things and may you remember their possible purpose.

And, as Papa Joe has always said, "Take your life one day at a time with a smile on your face, a positive attitude and don't sweat the little things."

What is a Senior Citizen? – March 1, 2013

To the editor:

In 1993, when I was writing my "Letter of Love to my Grandkids" book, I had a little dissertation on who or what is a senior citizen? I thought readers would enjoy what I wrote to my grandchildren.

What is a senior citizen? Well Little Dumplings let me tell you. A senior citizen is a person who was here before TV (can you believe that?), penicillin, polio shots, antibiotics, open heart surgery and hair implants. Before frozen foods (what in the world did we live on?), nylon, Dacron, Xerox, Kinsey (you'll have to ask your mom about his guy), fluorescent lights, credit cards (you're kidding Papa Joe!), ballpoint pens and Frisbees.

Yep, in the good old days "time sharing" meant togetherness, not computers or condos. We didn't have drip dry clothes, ice makers or dish washers. Coeds never wore slacks. We were before panty hose, clothes dryers, freezers and electric blankets.

We were here before men wore long hair and ear rings and before women wore tuxedos. We even got married first and then lived together. (How quaint, eh?) We were here before 40-hour work weeks and minimum wages.

Closets were for clothes, not for coming out of. We were before vitamins, disposable diapers, jeeps, pizza, face lifts, Cheerios, instant coffee, decaffeinated anything and believe it or not, no McDonald's! Back in our day, we thought fast food was what we ate for Lent. We were before FM radios, tape recorders, electric typewriters, VCRs, word processors, electronic music and disco dancing and karaoke.

When we were young, cigarette smoking was fashionable, grass for mowing. Coke was a refreshing drink and pot was something you cooked in. If you asked us what CIA, VCR, GNP, MBA, FFL, etc. meant, we would have said alphabet soup.

Well, what do you think Little Darlings? No, I'm not complaining. It was just like our food rations at home for our meals when we were kids. If you never had something, how can you miss it?

I do believe most of our senior citizens are a hardy bunch, especially when you stop to think how our world has changed and all the adjustments we have had to make and as the old saying goes, "We shall overcome" and with the help of the good Lord, I think we did!

Now it is time for Papa Joe to get a little philosophical and give you guys some words of wisdom. When you get to be Papa Joe's age, you do a lot of wondering and thinking. I know my time is running out so I have to make the best of my time from now on. To help me I have put a note on the fridge door that says, "If this was the last day of my life, what would I want to accomplish more than anything else?" I'll tell you one thing, that statement keeps my mind active and thinking and tells me: "Joe, keep going, you have a lot to do yet in life, but you are running out of time." It truly has been a motivational factor for me and something you Little Darlings should think about as you grow up.

What if it was announced that the world was coming to an end in an hour, what would you do? Personally, I think there would be a long line before each and every telephone with people waiting to call other people, especially their loved ones to tell them how much they missed them and how much they loved them. I also think there would be a big group moaning and mourning: "Why didn't I do the this and why didn't I do that and why didn't I do the things li always wanted to do?"

See what I mean? Don't wait for that last hour, it could come before you're ready. Do what you want to do (within the law and good conscience!) and especially remember to tell your loved ones how much you love them. Don't be ashamed or embarrassed or try to wait until the right time or use fancy phrases. All you have to do is say, "I love you."

So, stop what you're doing right now, including reading this letter. Who is nearest to you as you read this? Give them a big hug and tell them how much you love them. (I hope you're not in the library or in a class with a couple of dozen other students!)

Seriously, we often take our loved ones for granted and forget to tell them how much we love them. So, don't delay, do it today! Remember, a hug or two a day helps keep the blues away! Don't forget your old Papa Joe who loves you tons and tons!

Some Easter Memories – March 31, 2013

To the editor:

I did not partake in all the celebrations and drinking of green beer, on St. Patrick's Day, but I sure did partake in all the corned beef and cabbage I could get. It's one of my favorite meals.

Probably unknown to a lot of you is that March 19 was St. Joseph Day, my patron saint's namesake day. No, I don't celebrate that day by drinking and eating, but I do celebrate it in my own way. I kneel by the side of my bed and in my prayer I thank St. Joseph for all the wonderful care and help he gave to the blessed Virgin Mary in the child birth of Jesus. Wonderful story!

I am also especially thankful to St. Joseph for all the help and support I have asked him for and received in 88 wonderful years in this wonderful world.

Now that Christ has risen, it is Easter time and time for some old memories. Many years ago, when Margie and I decided to get married, I thought it would be a good idea for Margie to meet my mother and family in Terre Haute, Ind., my hometown. When I picked her up in Buffalo to head home, she had a large box with her suitcase. When I questioned her, she said it was an Easter present for me, with Easter being the following weekend.

I begged Margie to tell me what it was until she finally gave in and gave the present to me. It was a huge white chocolate Easter bunny. Huge! I chewed on it for weeks! That's one of my all-time favorite Easter memories.

In my letter of love to my grandchildren that I wrote back in the early '90s, I found the following dissertation that I gave to them.

"Went to 9 a.m. mass and as is usual on Easter Sunday, the church was packed with people standing all around the newly renovated and beautiful St. Ann's Catholic Church. I call these people the 'Once a year church goers' because most of them only go to church once a year. Maybe twice a year – some of them also go to church on Christmas. Too bad! Isn't it a shame that people can't take one hour a week to go to God's house, to visit and talk with him? If it were their work boss's house, they would go three-four times a week and probably spend several hours each visit. Well I got news for you and don't you forget it – God is the boss! So take a little of your time each day, even if only for a couple of minutes, and visit with him or at least talk to him. P.S. And don't forget to thank him for everything he has done for you and given you – everything!

Happy Easter to everyone!

Lonely – March 22, 2013

To the editor:

Are you lonely tonight? Do you miss your loved ones and old friends? As you age, day by day, a lot of your loved ones have moved away or to a nursing home or worse yet, passed away. OK, you're thankful you're not one of them. But the more of them you lose, the lonelier you become.

Are you lonely tonight? Yes, I'm lonely, especially since I lost my spouse of many years. No one to talk to, no one to eat with, no one to sleep with. Yes, it would be very nice to hold that loved one in my arms and say "I love you." Wouldn't that be wonderful?

Yes, those are some of the unfortunate feelings we experience if we have lived a longer life. We not only experience loneliness, but a lot of tribulations with health problems. And not too many good friends we can confide in or tell them our woes. Or ask for help and advice.

I guess life wouldn't be so lonely if it wasn't so redundant and repetitive. Morning time: Don't want to get out of bed. Why? I don't have anything to do and no place to go. So, what will I do? Go outside for the morning paper, shower and shave and dress.

What's for breakfast this morning? The usual – oatmeal cooked with a sliced banana and some raisins and crushed walnuts. Really good for me, but I had that yesterday. How about some shredded wheat or Cheerios? I had that the day before!

Showered, shaved and fed and read the paper. Now what do I do to conquer my world? I know, I'll take my usual morning walk and take the iPod one of my daughters gave to me. It's loaded with all those good old timers, Tony Martin, Frank Sinatra, Bing Crosby, Perry Como, etc. Cool! I don't listen to any radio news – it will disturb my thoughts and prayers.

Back home refreshed and rejuvenated, now what do I do? Wash the breakfast and last night's dinner dishes. Not too many of them as TV dinners are compact and pretty well contained. Just the salad dish, fruit dish and silverware. Oh yes, the wine glass! Man cannot live on bread alone and they say a glass of red wine is healthy for me.

Oh, I forgot one thing. When I'm walking, at any time, I turn my music down and say my morning prayers. I thank God, Jesus, Mary, St. Anthony and St. Jude for all the help and support on getting me through this wonderful lonely life of mine. Holy Mackeral forgive me, I just about forgot my good buddy St. Joseph!

Now that the bed is made, the dishes are done, and it's only 9 o'clock, what do I do until lunch time? Well, if it's summer time, I go out and cut the grass, trim the bushes and shrubs, weed the garden and fertilize the flowers and vegetable garden.

That gets me to lunch time. Any leftovers from last night? No, dinner last night was the leftovers from the night before. Maybe I'll treat myself and go out for a sandwich. Don't know how good the sandwich will be but I may see some of my old friends out and about and that will cheer me up.

After lunch I have to think about my nap time – generally 40 minutes. My doctor told me if I take an hour nap every day I could live another five years. I told him that meant I was going to live to 105 because I was already planning to live 100 years. So I'm going to stick with the 40-minute nap, I don't want to sleep my life away.

Yes, I am very happy and reasonably healthy and I thank God every morning, noon and night for what he has given me. But I still get very lonely from time to time and so do your loved ones!

Your spouses know you love them, but you should tell them more often. "If I just had one more chance" is one of the worst things to hear yourself say – then it's already too late. So please tell your loved one you love him or her today! You never know, it could be the last chance you get!

"I love you" is the sweetest music a person can hear. A bouquet of flowers smell the sweetest when they are in the hands of the recipient – not stacked by their casket! And praise is most appreciated when it can be heard by the person who earned it – not when it is recited in a eulogy or after he or she has passed away. So speak up before it's too late!

I would like to urge readers to include those who are alone through divorce or widowhood in their celebration of the Easter season. Make it a season in which they, too, can feel special, loved and part of things rather than isolated, forgotten and alone. And don't stop there – all holidays can be lonely for those who have lost loved ones. Include them in all of your holiday plans and you will be blessed and they will be blessed knowing that someone cares.

Words of Advice – April 11, 2013

To the editor:

I feel a little frisky today, so I think I should pass on some recent words of wisdom I have gathered. I also want to share with you an experience I encountered about drinking and driving. Beware! But first, the words of wisdom.

- People who live in glass houses should make love in the basement.
- Never read the fine print. There ain't no way you're going to like it.
- If you let a smile be your umbrella, then most likely your butt will get soaking wet.
- The only two things we do with greater frequency in middle age are urinate and attend funerals.

- The trouble with bucket seats is that not everybody has the same size bucket.
- To err is human, to forgive – highly unlikely.
- Money can't buy happiness, but somehow it's more comfortable to cry in a Porsche than in a Hyundai.
- Drinking makes some husbands see double and feel single.
- Living in a nudist colony takes all the fun out of Halloween.
- After a certain age, if you don't wake up aching in every joint, you are probably dead.
- I hate those hoax warnings, but this one is important! Send this warning to everyone on your e-mail list! If someone comes to your front door saying they are conducting a survey and asks you to take your clothes off, DO NOT DO IT! This is a scam; they only want to see you naked. I wish I'd gotten this yesterday. I feel so stupid and cheap now.

And now I would like to share an experience with you about drinking and driving.

As you well know, some of us have been lucky not to have had brushes with the authorities on our way home from the various social sessions over the years.

A couple of nights ago, I was out for a few drinks with some friends and had a few too many beers and then topped it off with a margarita. Not a good idea.

Knowing full well I was at least slightly over the limit, I did something I've never done before: I took a taxi home.

Sure enough I passed a police road block but because it was a taxi, they waved it past.

I arrived home safely without incident, which was a real surprise.

I have never driven a taxi before and am not sure where I got it.

P.S. Only kidding. I just had to pass on this little made up story. About the only drinking Papa Joe does these days is prune juice and carrot juice.

Precious Memories – April 25, 2013

To the editor:

Many years ago, a good "blood bank" buddy of mine sent me the following story to remind me of "Life." I can no longer keep it in my file of favorite stories so I am passing it on for your enlightenment and enjoyment. I think you'll enjoy it.

A little girl had been shopping with her Mom in a department store. She must have been 6 years old, this beautiful red haired, freckle faced image of innocence. It was pouring rain outside. The kind of rain that gushes over the top of rain gutters, so much in a hurry to hit the earth it has no time to flow down the spout. We all stood there under the awning and just inside the door of the store.

We waited, some patiently, others irritated because nature messed up their hurried day. I am always mesmerized by rainfall – I got lost in the sound and sight of the heavens washing away the dirt and dust of the world. Memories of running, splashing to carefree as a child came pouring in as a welcome reprieve from the worries of my day.

The little voice was so sweet as it broke the hypnotic trance we were all caught in: "Mom, let's run through the rain," she said.

"What?" Mom asked.

"Let's run through the rain," she repeated.

"No honey. We'll wait until it slows down a bit," Mom replied.

This young child waited about another minute and repeated: "Mom, let's run through the rain."

"We'll get soaked if we do," Mom said.

"No, we won't Mom. That's not what you aid this morning," the young girl said as she tugged at her Mom's arm.

"This morning? When did I say we could run through the rain and not get wet?"

"Don't you remember? When you were talking to Daddy about his cancer, you said 'If God can get us through this, he can get us through anything!'"

The entire crowd stopped dead silent. I swear you couldn't hear anything but the rain. We all stood silently.

No one came or left in the next few minutes.

Mom paused and thought for a moment about what she would say. Now some would laugh it off and scold her for being silly. Some might even ignore what was said. But this was a moment of affirmation in a young child's life. A time when innocent trust can be nurtured so that it will bloom into faith.

"Honey, you are absolutely right. Let's run through the rain. If God lets us get wet, well maybe we just needed washing," Mom said.

Then off they ran. We all stood watching, smiling and laughing as they darted past the cars and yes, through the puddles. They held their shopping bags over their heads just in case. They got soaked. But they were followed by a few who screamed and laughed like children all the way to their cars. And yes, I did. I ran. I got wet. I needed washing.

Circumstances or people can take away your material possessions, they can take away your money, and they can take away your health. But no one can ever take away your precious memories ... So, don't forget to make time and take the opportunities to make memories every day. To everything there is a season and a time to every purpose under heaven.

P.S. I hope you take the time to run through the rain!

They say it takes a minute to find a special person, an hour to appreciate them, a day to love them, but an entire life to forget them. Send this to someone you'll never forget. If you don't send it to someone, it means you're in a hurry. Take the time to live! Keep in touch with your friend. You never know when you'll need each other – and don't forget to run through the rain!

On Outhouses, Oatmeal – May 22, 2013

To the editor:

I have written several dissertations about the good old days, but what were they really like for Papa Joe in Terre Haute, Ind., as a kid? Let's start out with my outhouse experience as a kid.

Now, for the benefit of you modern folks, what is an outhouse? Well, it's a small wooden structure, also know as a privy or earth closet, which covers a pit toilet. Got it?

The outhouse was normally a two or three "seater," depending on the family. One seat was a low sitting and small hole for the kids, so they wouldn't fall in. The other two seats were higher sitting and the holes were larger to accommodate the older kids and adults. Since we didn't have Charmin or any of those other fancy toilet tissues in those days, our most prominent toilet tissue was a Sears Roebuck catalog. Just think what it might have been like in those days without a Sears catalog!

Now you are probably wondering what we did in the middle of the night when we had to go to the bathroom. Well, we had a "bed pan" that everyone used during the night. Then, in the morning, some unlucky person was delegated the job of emptying the bedpan out in the outhouse.

Try to imagine what it was like to wake up in the morning and the first thing you have to do is go potty. Also, you are still in your underwear (we didn't have nor could mom afford to buy us pajamas) and the outside temperature is in the freeze zone with maybe a little snow on the ground. So, what do you do now? Put on your clothes and shoes and make that LONG walk in the cold and snow to the outhouse. And then deal with the torture of that cold seat!

But old Papa Joe was no dummy. He learned how to beat the system at an early school age. When he started going to school at St. Benedict's, they had "inside" toilets — in a heated room! So the thing to do was to get up early, get out of bed, get dressed as quickly as possible, eat a bowl of cereal (eat your oatmeal Joe, my mother used to say, it will stick to your ribs. That meant it was good for you!) and then take off for school as fast as he could — so he could use that inside toilet in the heated room.

The priest and nuns at St. Benedict's thought I was a really eager young man because I was always the first kid to school every day. The only thing they couldn't figure out was how come such an eager kid was only getting "fair" grades. I guess I was a slow learner — about some things.

That experience was one of the reasons for my philosophy on life — Take life one day at a time, with a positive attitude, a smile on my face and DON'T SWEAT THE LITTLE THINGS!

The Green Thing – June 12, 2013

To the editor:

Why is it that every time we think things are running smoothly, someone throws a fly in the ointment. Or the shopping bag.

The other day as I was checking out at one of the local grocery stores, the young grocery clerk suggested to the older lady in front of me that she should bring her own grocery shopping bags because plastic bags were not good for the environment.

The woman explained, "We didn't have this green thing in my earlier days."

The clerk responded, "That's why we have our problem today, your generation did not care enough to save our environment."

He was right, our generation didn't have the green thing in our earlier days to help save the environment.

Back in my earlier days, we returned milk bottles, soda bottles and beer bottles to the store. The store then sent them back to the plant to be washed and sterilized and refilled so they could be used over and over. So, they were really recycled.

But, we did not have the green thing back in our day!

Back then, we washed the baby diapers because we did not have the throw away kind. We dried the diapers on an outside clothes line because we did not have an energy burning machine burning up to 220 volts-wind and solar power dried our clothing.

Back then we didn't fire up an engine and burn gasoline just to cut the lawn. We used a hand pushed mower that ran on human power.

We exercised by working so we didn't have to go to a health club to run on a treadmill that operates on electricity.

But he was right, we didn't have the Green thing back then.

Back then the people took the streetcar or a bus, and the kids rode their bikes to school instead of their moms turning into a 24-hour taxi service.

Bur isn't it sad the current generation laments how wasteful we folks were just because we didn't have the Green Thing back then.

Folks, please pass this information on to any other selfish, old person who needs a lesson in conservation from a smart—young person. Remember, don't make old people mad. We don't like being old in the first place. So it doesn't take too much to tick us off.

Chocolate is the Best – June 25, 2013

To the editor:

For the benefit of my friends, I am going to admit or confess that I have been a member of the AACL for many years. A charter member, that is, and the organization is the American Association of Chocolate Lovers. Naturally we have rules and regulations we must abide by. Since you are edification-seeking friends, I am passing these tidbits on to you for your acknowledgement and enjoyment. Here goes ...

THE RULES OF CHOCOLATE

- If you have chocolate all over your hands, you're eating it too slowly.
- Chocolate covered raisins, cherries, orange slices and strawberries all count as fruit, so eat as many as you want.
- The problem: How to get two pounds of chocolate home from the store in a hot car. The solution: Eat it in the parking lot.
- Diet tip: Eat a chocolate bar before each meal. It'll take the edge off your appetite and you'll eat less.
- A nice box of chocolates can provide your total daily intake of calories in one place. Isn't that handy?
- If you can't eat all of your chocolate, it will keep in the freezer. But if you can't eat all of your chocolate, what's wrong with you?

- If calories are an issue, store your chocolate on top of the fridge. Calories are afraid of heights, and they will jump out of the chocolate to protect themselves.
- If I eat equal amounts of dark chocolate and white chocolate, is that a balanced diet? Don't they actually counteract each other?
- Money talks, chocolate sings.
- Chocolate has many preservatives. Preservatives make you look younger.
- Q: Why is there no such organization as Chocoholics Anonymous? A: Because no one wants to quit.

Put "eat chocolate" at the top of your list of things to do today. That way, at least you'll get one thing done. There, all is said and done and now it's up to you to follow up and take the ball, chocolate that is, and do what you have to do. Follow the rules and regulations and you, too, will be a member in good standing. Welcome!

Some Gems That Will Help Improve Your Day — July 18, 2013

To the editor:

Many years ago, too many to mention, when I was still employed, one of my responsibilities was to write a monthly report highlighting the department's activities and performance. Sometimes things weren't too "cheerful" so, in an effort to lighten things up, I would include in my reports some words of wisdom, or as I called them, some Gems of the Day. Here are some of them — enjoy!

- By the time you stop to smell the roses, some idiot has already spread the fertilizer.
- Never tell your wife her nylons are wrinkled — unless you know for a fact that she's wearing nylons.
- Have you noticed that very few people go to the doctor when they have a cold or cough? They go to the theater or concert and sit next to you.
- What is the best thing to do when the brakes fail while you are driving? Hit something soft.
- One of the tests of your true religion is when you are in church with nothing less than a $20 bill.
- Here's a suggestion for those who want to lose weight — put the bathroom scale in front of the refrigerator.
- I have needed glasses since the day I tried to dial the pencil sharpener.
- You don't have to go to medical school to learn that lending money to relatives can cause amnesia.
- Help a man when he's in trouble and you can be sure he'll remember you — when he gets in trouble again.
- If it weren't for the fact that the TV and refrigerator are in different rooms, we probably wouldn't get any exercise at all.

OK, I hope you're smiling, Just one final comment. Before I could finish this letter, my computer stopped and I had to get a new mouse. So, here's my final Gem of the Day:

Things to do tomorrow ... Get up at the crack of dawn, stuff up the crack, go back to bed.

ABOUT THE AUTHOR

Joseph Herman Anthony Lubbehusen, better known as Papa Joe, was born in Terre Haute, Indiana on October 20, 1924 to Philomena Oser Lubbehusen. He attended St. Benedicts School until graduating from the 8th grade and then attended Mt. St. Francis Seminary to study for the priesthood. In his third year of Seminary, WW2 broke out and he was drafted and inducted in the U.S. Army where he spent 3 years in the 84th Infantry, 3rd Army under Gen. George Patton.

After the war, Joe returned to Terre Haute and attended Indiana State College and the American Institute of Baking in Chicago. Joe was hired by the Dow Corning Corporation as a technical service representative in the Cleveland Territory and spent nearly 39 years with Dow Corning Corporation in various managerial positions.

Upon retirement, Joe coordinated the Dow Corning Ernie Wallace Blood Bank program for 25 years. He was a 160 pint donor until a bout with cancer ended his eligibility to donate blood.

In his younger days, Joe was an avid bowler and golfer. At one time he held the third highest bowling average in his home town of Midland, Michigan, but the years took its toll and Papa Joe, as he has come to be known to his friends and family, has lost most of his ability and agility needed for bowling and golfing. (Only for golfing and bowling though!)

Joe is a 60-year member of the Midland Lions Club and still very active in the Alzheimer's Association. He resides in Midland, Michigan.